KOIGU

wrapped in color

wrapped in color
30 shawls to knit

KOIGU HANDPAINTED YARNS
MAIE LANDRA & TAIU LANDRA

sixth&springbooks
NEW YORK

sixth&springbooks

161 Avenue of the Americas
New York, NY 10013
sixthandspringbooks.com

Managing Editor
LAURA COOKE

Senior Editor
LISA SILVERMAN

Art Director
DIANE LAMPHRON

Yarn Editor
VANESSA PUTT

Editorial Assistant
JOHANNA LEVY

Supervising
Patterns Editor
LORI STEINBERG

Patterns Editors
LISA BUCCELLATO
LORETTA DACHMAN

Still Photography
MARCUS TULLIS

Model Photography
JACK DEUTSCH

Fashion Stylist
JOANNA RADOW

Assistant Stylist
JENNA SLEVIN

Hair & Makeup
SOKPHALLA BAN

Vice President
TRISHA MALCOLM

Publisher
CAROLINE KILMER

Production Manager
DAVID JOINNIDES

President
ART JOINNIDES

Chairman
JAY STEIN

Copyright © 2015 by Maie Landra and Taiu Landra

Library of Congress Cataloging-in-Publication Data

Wrapped in color : 30 shawls to knit in Koigu handpainted
yarn / Maie Landra and Taiu Landra — First edition.
    pages cm
ISBN 978-1-936096-84-8
1. Knitting—Patterns. 2. Shawls. 3. Dyes and dyeing—
Wool. 4. Color in clothing. I. Koigu Wool Designs (Firm)
TT825.W73 2014
746.43'2—dc23

                                2014027170

MANUFACTURED IN CHINA

1 3 5 7 9 10 8 6 4 2

First Edition

◆
Grateful
thanks to
EILEEN FISHER
for providing
some garments
for styling.

◆ The shawl pictured
at right is **Keepsake**
(page 90), knitted in the
following colorways of
KPPPM: #P612 (A),
#P816 (B), #P511L (C),
#P814 (D), #P605 (E),
#P608 (F), #P621 (G),
#P513 (H), #P602 (I),
#P628 (J), #P623 (K),
and #P324 (L).

◆ TO MY LATE MOTHER,
LEIDA KIILASPEA.
—MAIE LANDRA

Contents

Introduction 9

Charlotte's Daughter Nellie 12

Alligator 16

Rhapsody in Color 18

Valentina 21

Charlotte's Web 25

Peek-a-Boo 30

Starfish 32

Patch of Berries 36

Charlotte's Daughter Joy 38

Allusion 41

Groovy 44

Waves 46

Tumble Leaves 49

Dash 53

Lucky Lady 56

Victoria 61

Stroke of Midnight 64

Elizabeth 66

Maria 69

Metamorphosis Shrug 72

Gypsy 75

Woodsong 79

Corinne 84

Silver Lace 87

Keepsake 90

Tabitha 94

Kiki 96

Cobweb 98

Lola 100

Rihanna 102

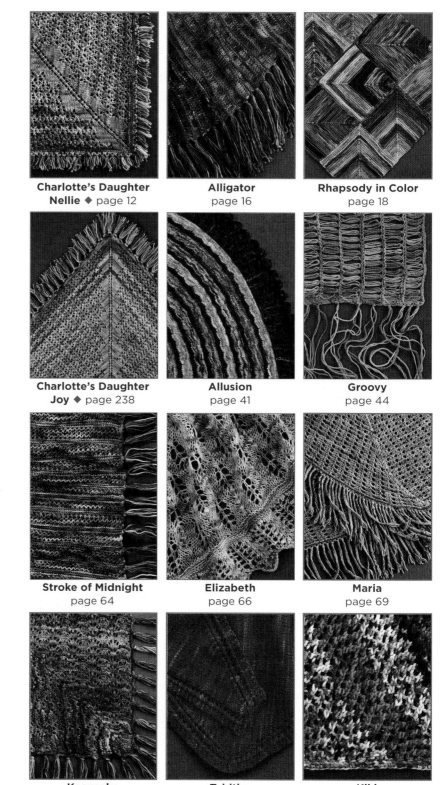

Charlotte's Daughter Nellie ◆ page 12

Alligator page 16

Rhapsody in Color page 18

Charlotte's Daughter Joy ◆ page 238

Allusion page 41

Groovy page 44

Stroke of Midnight page 64

Elizabeth page 66

Maria page 69

Keepsake page 90

Tabitha page 94

Kiki page 96

Valentina
page 21

Charlotte's Web
page 25

Peek-a-Boo
page 30

Starfish
page 32

Patch of Berries
page 36

Waves
page 46

Tumble Leaves
page 49

Dash
page 53

Lucky Lady
page 56

Victoria
page 61

Metamorphosis Shrug
page 72

Gypsy
page 75

Woodsong
page 79

Corinne
page 84

Silver Lace
page 77

Cobweb
page 98

Lola
page 100

Rihanna
page 102

Tools & Techniques **105**

Resources **110**

Acknowledgments **111**

Further Readings **111**

Index **112**

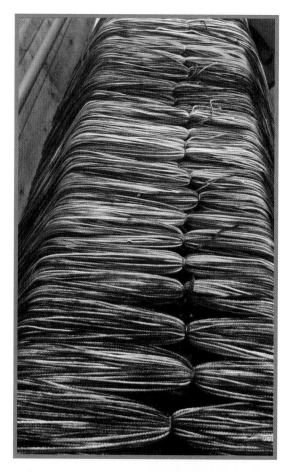

Introduction

Koigu: the name suggests a fantastic kingdom, or an exotic breed of sheep. In truth, it is the farm and yarn company of Maie Landra, her daughter Taiu, and her granddaughter Kersti; the name honors the ancestral Estonian home of Maie's late husband. The beauty of the family's farmland is reflected in the yarn produced there—in the world of Koigu color.

Now *Wrapped in Color* brings you 30 gorgeous knitted shawl projects inspired by that color and the joy it brings. Maie and Taiu's mission for Koigu was to produce fine, soft merino yarn painted by hand in small batches—each skein a painter's palette. Where some designers might use a dozen colors in a sweater, Maie would use a dozen in a single skein, creating a range of colorways the likes of which knitters had never imagined.

At first, each skein was an adventure. Then Maie and Taiu began to record their creations in a book whose secrets no outside observer could decipher. They use that system to this day and now have more than 400 colorways, inspired by every nuance of every season. The quantities for each dye lot are small, and the results reflect the environment and the personality of the dyer. The shawls in this book, many designed by the Landras, use a range of stitch patterns and constructions to show off those palettes in stunning ways.

Today Koigu fans can choose among several yarns: KPPPM; Kersti, a DK-weight merino crepe; Koigu Bulky Merino; Koigu Merino Lace; and Koigu Mori, a mix of merino and mulberry silk. This book includes projects using all these yarns, in patterns from lace to garter stitch, from delicate, ethereal wraps to cozy capes. Knitters of every skill level will find inspiration to create their own works of wearable art, out of the art that is Koigu. ◆

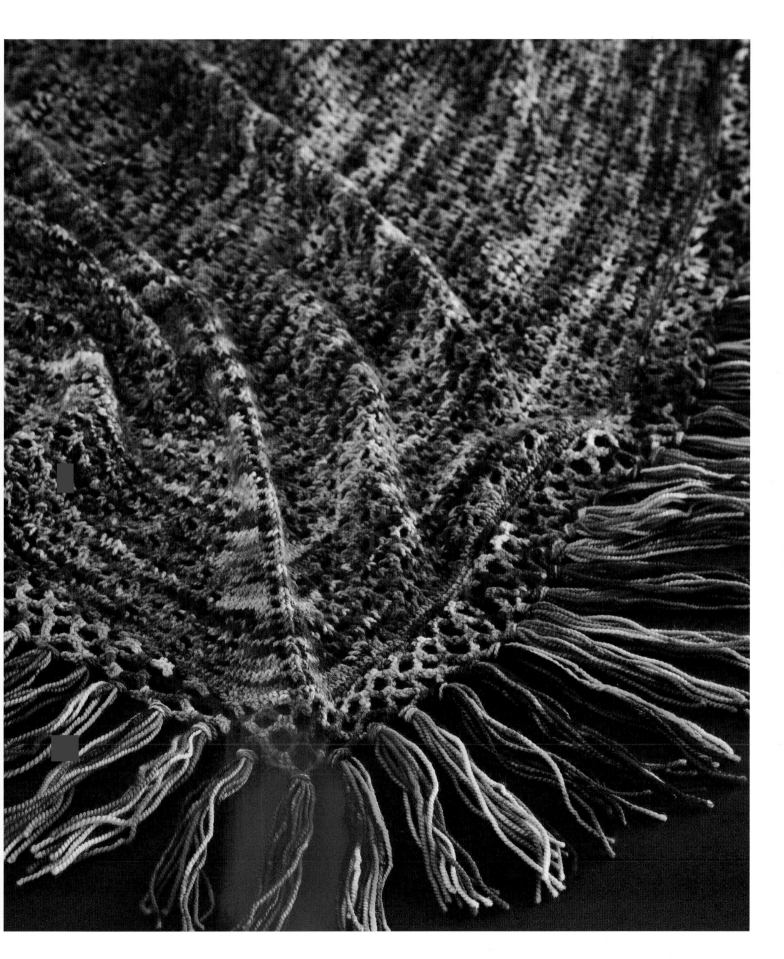

the projects

Charlotte's Daughter Nellie

Nellie, along with her sister shawl, Joy, is knitted in five different variegated colorways. See the cover for an alternate version!

MEASUREMENTS
◆ Width after blocking 64"/162.5cm
◆ Length from back neck to center point after blocking 27"/68.5cm

MATERIALS
◆ One 1¾oz/50g skein (each 175yd/161m) of Koigu *KPPPM* (merino wool) each in #P300 (A), #P314 (B), #P303L (C), #P130 (D), and P138 (E) **[1]**

◆ Size 3 (3.25mm) circular needle, 32"/80cm long (used to work back and forth), *or size to obtain gauge*

◆ Size D/3 (3.25mm) crochet hook

◆ 2 stitch markers

GAUGE
24 stitches and 34 rows = 4"/10cm over lace pattern after blocking using size 3 (3.25mm) needle.
TAKE TIME TO CHECK GAUGE.

STRIPE PATTERN
2 rows A, 2 rows B, 2 rows A, 24 rows B.
[2 rows C, 2 rows B] twice, 24 rows C.
[2 rows D, 2 rows C] twice, 24 rows D.
[2 rows E, 2 rows D] twice, 24 rows E.
[2 rows B, 2 rows E] twice, 8 rows B, 2 rows A.

NOTE
Shawl is worked from the center of the neck to the lower point.

SHAWL
With A, cast on 7 sts. Knit 1 row, purl 1 row.
Next (inc) row (RS) Sl 1, k1, yo, k1, yo, place marker (pm), k1 (center st), pm, yo, k to last 2 sts, yo, k2—11 sts.
Next row (WS) Sl 1, p to end, sl markers.
Next (inc) row (RS) Sl 1, k1, yo, k to 1 st before marker, yo, sl marker, k1, sl marker, yo, k to last 2 sts, yo, k2—4 sts inc'd.
Next row Sl 1, p to end.
Rep last 2 rows 5 times more—35 sts.

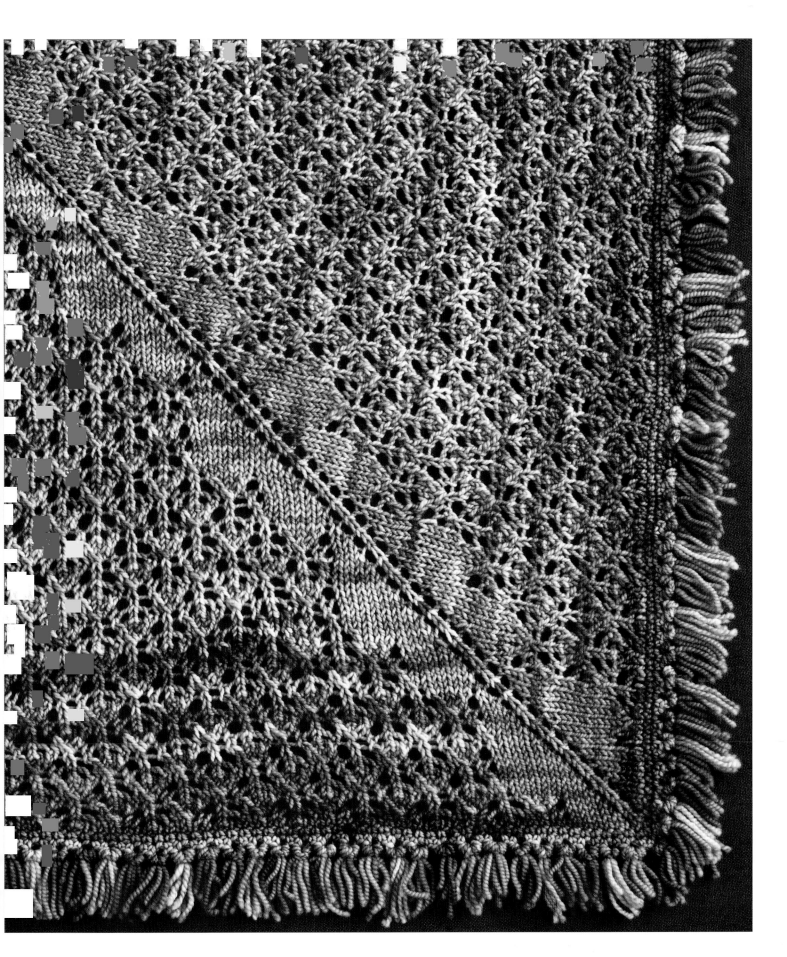

Charlotte's Daughter Nellie

COVER VERSION
(pictured below)

COLORWAYS
◆ 1 skein each in
#P118B (B), #P151 (D),
and #P112 (E)
◆ 2 skeins each in
#P131 (A) and #P133 (C)

CROCHET EDGING
With A and crochet hook,
work 1 row of sc along
bound-off edge.
Row 2 Ch 3, sc in next sc,
*ch 6, sk 1 sc, sc in next
2 sc. Rep from *. Ch 3. Turn.
Rows 3-5 Ch 4, *2 sc in next
ch-6 sp, ch 6. Ch 3. Turn.
Fasten off at end of row 5.

FRINGE
Alternating A and C,
cut 5 strands of yarn
9"/23cm long. Holding
5 strands tog, fold in
half and with crochet
hook, draw loop through
first ch-6 space on
lower edge of shawl.
Draw ends of strands
through folded loop and
pull to tighten. Rep in
each ch-6 space along
lower edge of shawl.◆

BEGIN STRIPE PAT AND CHART
Row 1 With A, sl 1, k1, work row 1 of chart to marker, sl marker, k1, sl marker, work row 1 of chart to last 2 sts, k2—4 sts inc'd.
Row 2 Sl 1, p1, work row 2 of chart to marker, sl marker, k1, sl marker, work row 2 of chart to last 2 sts, p2. Cont to work chart in this way, foll stripe pat, through row 16. Cont in stripe pat as foll:
Next row (RS) Sl 1, k1, work row 1 of chart to rep line, work 6-st rep 3 times across, work to end of chart row, sl marker, k1, work row 1 of chart to rep line, work 6-st rep 3 times across, work to end of chart row, k2—4 sts inc'd.
Cont in this way, working 6-st rep twice more on each side of center st for every 16-row rep, until stripe pat is complete. See chart rows 17–23. Bind off loosely.

FINISHING
CROCHET EDGING
With A and crochet hook, work 1 row of sc along bound-off edge. Work evenly along the bound-off edge only as foll:
Next row Ch 2, *sc in next sc, ch 4, sc in next sc; rep from * to end. Fasten off.

BLOCKING
Soak shawl in warm water and pin to maximum size. Allow to dry.

FRINGE
Using colors randomly, cut 4 strands of yarn 3"/7.5cm long. Holding 4 strands tog, fold in half and with crochet hook, draw loop through 1 ch-4 space on wrong side of lower edge. Draw ends through loop and pull to tighten. Rep in each ch-4 sp along lower edge of shawl.◆

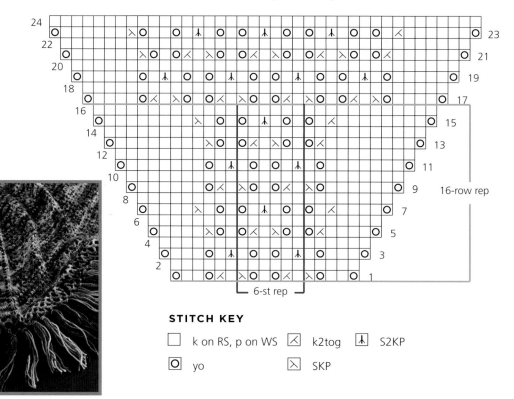

STITCH KEY

☐ k on RS, p on WS   ◹ k2tog   ⟰ S2PK

◉ yo   ◺ SKP

Alligator

Gorgeous jewel tones and an easy drop-stitch pattern make a long and lush wrap that can be doubled for extra warmth.

MEASUREMENTS
◆ Width 30"/76cm
◆ Length not including fringe 100"/254cm

MATERIALS
◆ Two 1¾oz/50g skeins
(each 175yd/160m) of Koigu KPPPM
(merino wool) each in #P816 (A),
#P426 (B), #P126 (C), #P511D (D),
and #P830 (E) **1**

◆ Size 3 (3.25mm) circular needle,
60"/150cm long (used to work back and
forth), *or size to obtain gauge*

◆ Size D/3 (3.25mm) crochet hook

GAUGE
28 stitches and 36 rows = 4"/10cm
over St st after blocking using size
3 (3.25mm) needle.
TAKE TIME TO CHECK GAUGE.

PATTERN STITCH
(over any number of sts)
Rows 1-4 Knit.
Row 5 (RS) Knit, wrapping yarn twice for
each st.
Row 6 Knit, dropping extra wraps.
Rep rows 1–6 for pattern st.

SHAWL
With A, cast on 400 sts. Knit 2 rows.

BEGIN PATTERN ST
Work pat st in colors as foll: 18 rows A, 6
rows B, 6 rows A, 18 rows B, 6 rows C,
6 rows B, 18 rows C, 6 rows D, 6 rows C,
18 rows D, 6 rows E, 6 rows D, 18 rows E.
With E, knit 2 rows. Bind off.

FINISHING
BLOCKING
Soak in warm water and hang sideways
from bound-off row, pinning frequently to
ensure a straight edge. Allow to dry.

FRINGE
Cut 1 strand of yarn in each color,
11"/28cm long. Holding 5 strands tog,
fold in half and with crochet hook, draw
loop through one st in garter band on side
edge. Draw ends through loop and pull to
tighten. Rep along both side edges. ◆

Rhapsody in Color

DESIGNED BY MAIE LANDRA

●●●○

Mini skeinettes in assorted hues are used to create mitered squares in a shawl that makes beautiful music with color.

MEASUREMENTS (after blocking)
◆ Width 15"/38cm
◆ Length 50"/127cm

MATERIALS
◆ 120 mini skeinettes (each 11yd/10m) of Koigu *KPPPM* and *KPM* (merino wool) in assorted colors (**1**)

◆ Size 3 (3.25mm) double-pointed needles *or size to obtain gauge*

◆ One removable marker

GAUGES
29 stitches and 56 rows = 4"/10cm over twisted garter st (knit through the back loop, every row) after blocking using size 3 (3.25mm) needles.
One square measures
5 x 5"/13 x 13cm square.
TAKE TIME TO CHECK GAUGES.

NOTES
1. Shawl is made up of mitered squares, which are worked by picking up and casting on stitches along previously worked squares.
2. Colors are used randomly and changed as each mini skeinette is used up.
3. Shawl is worked in twisted garter st (knit every row through the back loop).
4. Weave in ends as you go.

SHAWL—BASE ROW
SQUARE 1
Cast on 69 sts. Place a marker on the center st and move this marker up every row.
Row 1 (WS) K68tbl, p1.

Row 2 Sl 1 knitwise, ktbl to 1 st before marked st, remove marker, SK2P, replace marker on center st, ktbl to last st, p1—2 sts dec'd.
Row 3 Sl 1 knitwise, ktbl to last st, p1.
Rep rows 2 and 3 until 5 sts rem, then rep row 2 once more—3 sts.
Next row (WS) Sl 1, p2tog, psso. Leave loop on needle.

Rhapsody in Color

SQUARES 2 AND 3

Keeping loop on needle, pick up and k 34 sts more along LH edge of square just knit, cast on 34 sts—69 sts. Complete as for square 1.

When square 3 is complete, fasten off and break yarn.

RIGHT-LEANING MITER ROW

SQUARE 4

Beg at corner between squares 2 and 3, pick up and k 35 sts along upper edge of square 3, cast on 34 sts—69 sts. Complete as for square 1.

SQUARES 5 AND 6

Keeping loop on needle, pick up and k 34 sts along RH edge of square just worked, pick up and k 34 sts along upper edge of square in previous row—69 sts. Complete as for square 1.

LEFT-LEANING MITER ROW

SQUARE 7

Beg at corner between squares 5 and 6, pick up and k 34 sts along upper edge of square 6, cast on 34 sts—69 sts. Complete as for square 1.

SQUARES 8 AND 9

Pick up and k 34 sts along LH edge of square just knit, pick up and k 34 sts along upper edge of square in previous row—69 sts. Complete as for square 1.

When square 9 is complete, fasten off and break yarn.

Continue in this manner, alternating right- and left-leaning miter rows, until 10 rows of squares have been worked.

FINISHING

BLOCKING

Pin to measurements, spray with water. Allow to dry.❖

Valentina

Every detail of this capelet exudes elegance, from the asymmetric crescent shape to the delicate lace pattern that flows into a ruffled hem.

MEASUREMENTS (after blocking)
◆ Length of straight edge at end of RS rows, including ruffle 17½"/44.5cm

MATERIALS
◆ Four 1¾oz/50g skeins (each 292yd/267m) of Koigu *Lace Merino* (merino wool) in #L1180 ⓪

◆ Size 2 (2.75mm) circular needle, 40"/100cm long (used to work back and forth), *or size to obtain gauge*

◆ Stitch markers

GAUGE
32 stitches = 5"/12.5cm and 28 rows = 3"/7.5cm over chart 2 after blocking using size 2 (2.75mm) needle.
TAKE TIME TO CHECK GAUGE.

STITCH GLOSSARY
Cluster [K3tog tbl without dropping old sts from LH needle, yo] 3 times, k3tog tbl and drop old sts from LH needle—7 sts made from 3.
3-st dec Sl 2 sts tog knitwise, k2tog, pass sl sts over the k2tog.
Nupp ([K1, yo] 3 times, k1) into same st; in next row, p these 7 sts tog to complete nupp.

NOTE
Asymmetric shawl is knit from the top down, with charted increases.

SHAWL
NECK EDGE BORDER
Cast on 3 sts. Work 94 rows in St st (k on RS, p on WS).

Valentina

Next row (RS) K3, pick up and k 63 sts along side of border, then 3 sts along cast-on edge—69 sts.
Next row P2, place marker (pm), [p8, pm] 8 times, p3. Slip markers every row.

BEGIN CHART 1
Row 1 (RS) K3, work row 1 of chart 8 times across, k2.
Row 2 P2, work row 2 of chart 8 times across, p3.
Cont in this manner until row 24 is complete—197 sts.

BEGIN CHART 2
Row 1 (RS) K3, work row 1 of chart 8 times across, k2.
Row 2 P2, work row 2 of chart 8 times across, p3.
Cont in this manner until row 28 is complete.
Next row (RS) K3, [work row 1 to blue rep line, work stitch rep twice across, work to

end of chart] 8 times, k2.
Cont in this manner until row 28 is complete.
Rep rows 1–28 once more, then rows 1–18 once, adding an additional stitch rep in each section every time row 28 is complete—645 sts.
Remove markers.

BEGIN CHART 3
Row 1 (RS) Work to rep line, work stitch rep 39 times, work to end of chart.
Cont in this manner until row 27 is complete. Work row 28, binding off loosely.

FINISHING
BLOCKING
Wash and block piece well.
Allow to dry.◈

STITCH KEY

☐	k on RS, p on WS
◹	k2tog
◺	SKP
◉	yo
▨	no stitch
◿	SK2P
◸	k3tog
◮	3-st decrease
▽	make nupp
◬	complete nupp
⋎	cluster

CHART 3

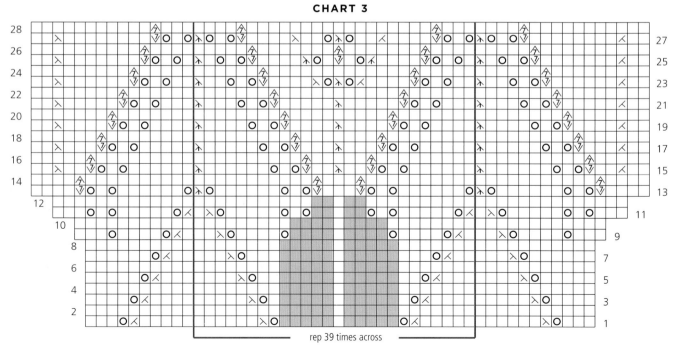

rep 39 times across

Valentina

CHART 1

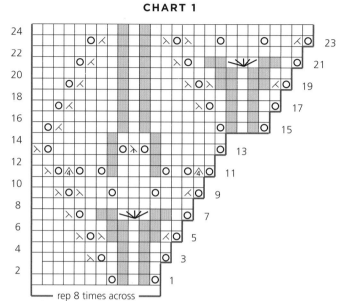

STITCH KEY

☐	k on RS, p on WS
⟋	k2tog
⟍	SKP
O	yo
▨	no stitch
⟑	SK2P
⟍	k3tog
④	3-st decrease
▽	make nupp
⟑	complete nupp
⤬⤬	cluster

CHART 2

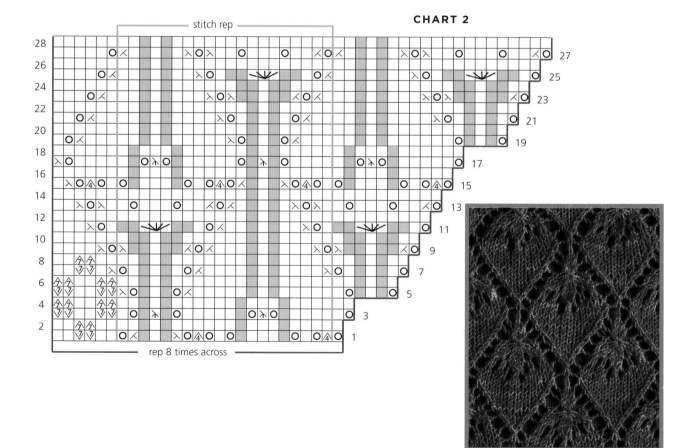

rep 8 times across

24

Charlotte's Web

The interplay of five colorways adds sophistication to a simple lace pattern. Knit all colorways the same width, or vary them to add a personal touch.

MEASUREMENTS
◆ Width 76"/193cm after blocking
◆ Length 38"/96cm after blocking

MATERIALS
◆ One 1¾oz/50g skein (each 175yd/161m) of Koigu KPPPM (merino wool) in #P319L (A), #P117 (B), #P314L (C), #P105L (D), and #P605 (E) ⓵

◆ Size 6 (4mm) circular needle, 40"/100cm long (used to work back and forth), *or size to obtain gauge*

◆ Size E/4 (3.5mm) crochet hook

◆ 2 stitch markers

GAUGE
16 stitches and 28 rows = 4"/10cm over lace pattern after blocking using size 6 (4mm) needle.
TAKE TIME TO CHECK GAUGE.

LACE PATTERN
(multiple of 8 sts plus 1)
Row 1 (RS) *K2, yo, SKP, k1, k2tog, yo, k1; rep from * to last st, k1.
Rows 2, 4, and 6 Purl.
Row 3 *K1, yo, SKP, yo, SK2P, yo, k2tog, yo; rep from * to end, k1.
Row 5 *[K1, yo, SK2P, yo] twice; rep from * to last st, k1.
Row 7 Rep row 5.
Row 8 Purl.
Rep rows 1–8 twice for lace pat.

STRIPE PATTERN
16 rows A.
[2 rows B, 2 rows A] for 16 rows.
16 rows B.
[2 rows C, 2 rows B] for 16 rows.
16 rows C.
[2 rows D, 2 rows C] for 16 rows.
16 rows D.
[2 rows E, 2 rows D] for 16 rows.
16 rows E.

Charlotte's Web

NOTES
1. Shawl is worked from the center of the neck to the lower point.
2. Lace pat may be worked from text or chart.

SHAWL
With A, cast on 7 sts.
Next row K3, place marker (pm), k1 (center st), pm, k to end.
Purl 1 row, slipping markers.
Next row (RS) K2, yo, k to marker, yo, sl marker, k1, sl marker, yo, k to last 2 sts, yo, k2—4 sts inc'd.
Next row Purl.
Rep last 2 rows 3 times more—23 sts.

BEGIN STRIPE PAT AND CHART
Row 1 (RS) With A, k2, work row 1 of chart to marker, sl marker, k1, sl marker, work row 1 of chart to marker, k2—4 sts inc'd.
Row 2 P2, work row 2 of chart to marker, sl marker, p1, sl marker, work row 2 of chart to marker, p2.
Cont to work chart in this way, changing colors for stripe pat, until row 16 is complete. Cont in stripe pat as foll:
Next row (RS) K2, work row 1 of chart to rep line, work 8-st rep 3 times across, work to end of chart row, sl marker, k1, work row 1 of chart to rep line, work 8-st rep 3 times across, work to end of chart row, k2—4 sts inc'd.
Cont in this way, working 8-st rep twice more on each side of center st for each 16-row rep, until stripe pat is complete. See chart rows 17–32. Bind off loosely.

FINISHING
CROCHET EDGING
With desired color and crochet hook, work 1 row in sc around entire shawl.
Work evenly along the bound-off edge only as foll:
Row 1 *Ch 9, skip 4 sc, sc into next sc; rep from * to end.
Row 2 *Ch 9, sc in next space; rep from * to end. Fasten off.

BLOCKING
Soak shawl in warm water and pin to maximum size. Allow to dry.

FRINGE
Using colors randomly, cut 5 strands of yarn, each 16"/41cm long. Holding 5 strands together, fold in half and with crochet hook, draw loop through one chain space on lower edge of shawl. Draw ends of strands through folded loop and pull to tighten. Rep in each ch-9 sp along lower edge of shawl.◈

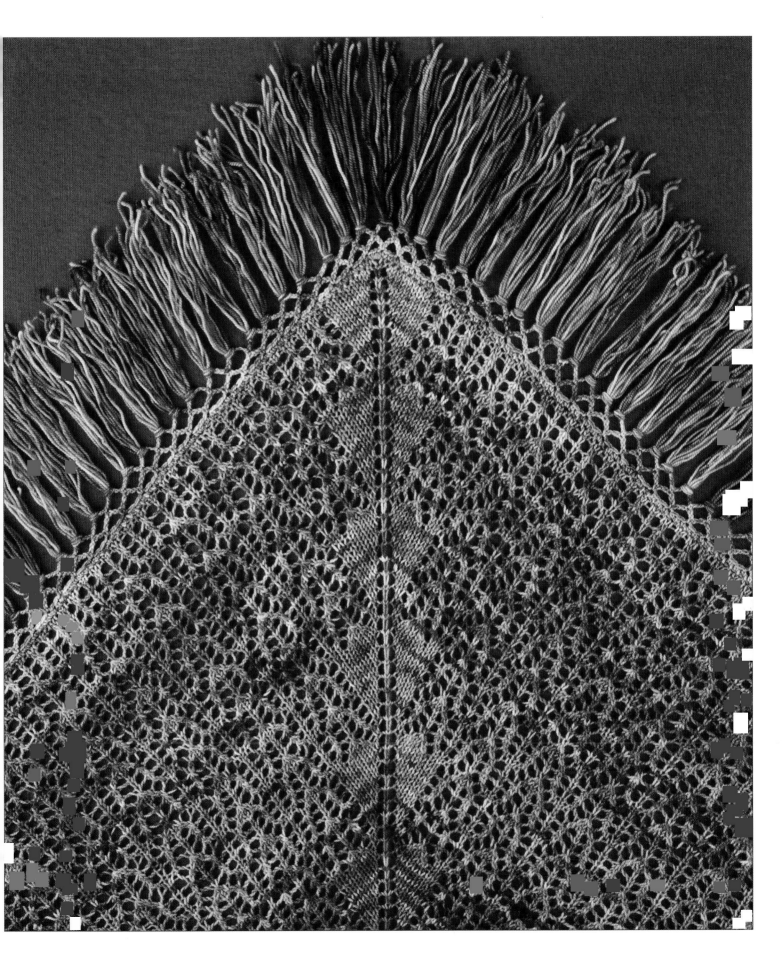

Charlotte's Web

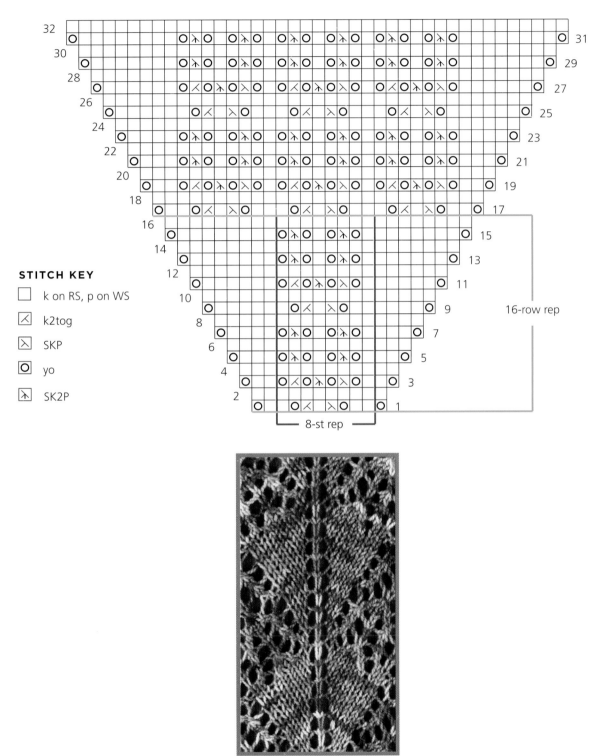

STITCH KEY

☐	k on RS, p on WS
◺	k2tog
◹	SKP
☉	yo
⋏	SK2P

16-row rep

8-st rep

Peek-a-Boo

Simplicity meets sumptuous silk and merino in an easy-to-knit lace shawl that drapes beautifully. A delicate crochet border is the perfect finishing touch.

MEASUREMENTS (after blocking)
◆ Width 20"/51cm
◆ Length not including crochet edging 78"/198cm

MATERIALS
◆ Six 1¾oz/50g skeins (each 185yd/169m) of Koigu *Mori* (merino wool/mulberry silk) in M303L **❶**

◆ One pair size 6 (4mm) needles *or size to obtain gauge*

◆ Size E/4 (3.5mm) crochet hook

GAUGE
19 stitches and 24 rows = 4"/10cm over lace pattern after blocking using size 6 (4mm) needles.
TAKE TIME TO CHECK GAUGE.

LACE PATTERN
(multiple of 4 sts plus 2)
Row 1 (RS) K1, *k2tog, [yo] twice, SKP; rep from * to last st, k1.
Row 2 and all WS rows Purl.
Row 3 Knit.
Row 5 K1, *[yo] twice, SKP, k2tog; rep from * to last st, k1.
Row 7 Knit.
Row 8 Purl.
Rep rows 1–8 for lace pat.

NOTE
Each yo counts as a stitch.

SHAWL
Cast on 94 sts. Knit 2 rows.
Work in lace pat until piece measures approx 78"/198cm from beg, end with a row 6. Knit 2 rows. Bind off.

FINISHING
CROCHET EDGING
With crochet hook, work 1 row of sc along cast-on edge of shawl.
Next row Ch 10, skip 3 sc, *sc in next 2 sc, ch 10, skip 2 sc; rep from * until 3 sc rem, ch 10, sc in last sc, turn.
Next 2 rows *Ch 10, sc twice in next ch-10 sp, rep from * to end, turn.
Fasten off.
Rep for bound-off edge of shawl.

BLOCKING
Wet shawl and pin to measurements.
Allow to dry. ◆

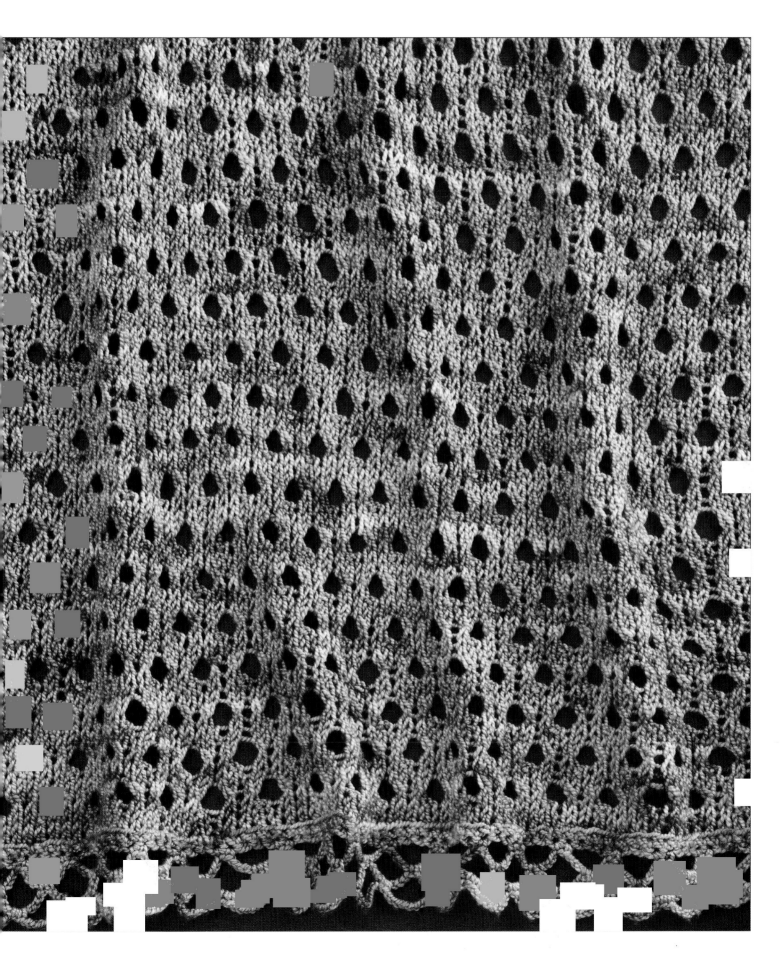

Starfish

Add sleeves to a generously sized wrap and you have an ingenious hybrid piece with exquisite details and numerous possibilities for creative styling.

SIZES
Sized for Small (Medium, Large)

MEASUREMENTS (after blocking)
◆ Width across back
14½ (16, 17½)"/37 (40.5, 44)cm
◆ Total width including borders
88 (89¼, 90½)"/223.5 (226.5, 230)cm
◆ Length at center back
19 (19½, 20)"/48 (49.5, 51)cm
◆ Upper arm
16¼ (17½, 18)"/ 41.5 (44.5, 45.5)cm

MATERIALS
◆ 9 (10, 11) 1¾oz/50g skeins
(each 175yd/161m) of Koigu *KPPPM*
(merino wool) in #P706D

◆ Size 3 (3.25mm) circular needle,
40"/100cm long (used to work back and
forth), *or size to obtain gauge*

◆ Size C/3 (3.25mm) crochet hook

GAUGE
18 stitches and 26 rows = 4"/10cm
over lace pattern after blocking using
size 3 (3.25mm) needles.
TAKE TIME TO CHECK GAUGE.

SHAWL
Cast on 319 (325, 331) sts. Knit 4 rows.

BEGIN CHART 1
Row 1 (RS) Work to rep line, work 6-st
rep 51 (52, 53) times across, work to
end of chart.
Cont to work in this manner until row
4 is complete. Rep rows 1–4 until piece
measures 9"/23cm from beg, end
with a WS row.

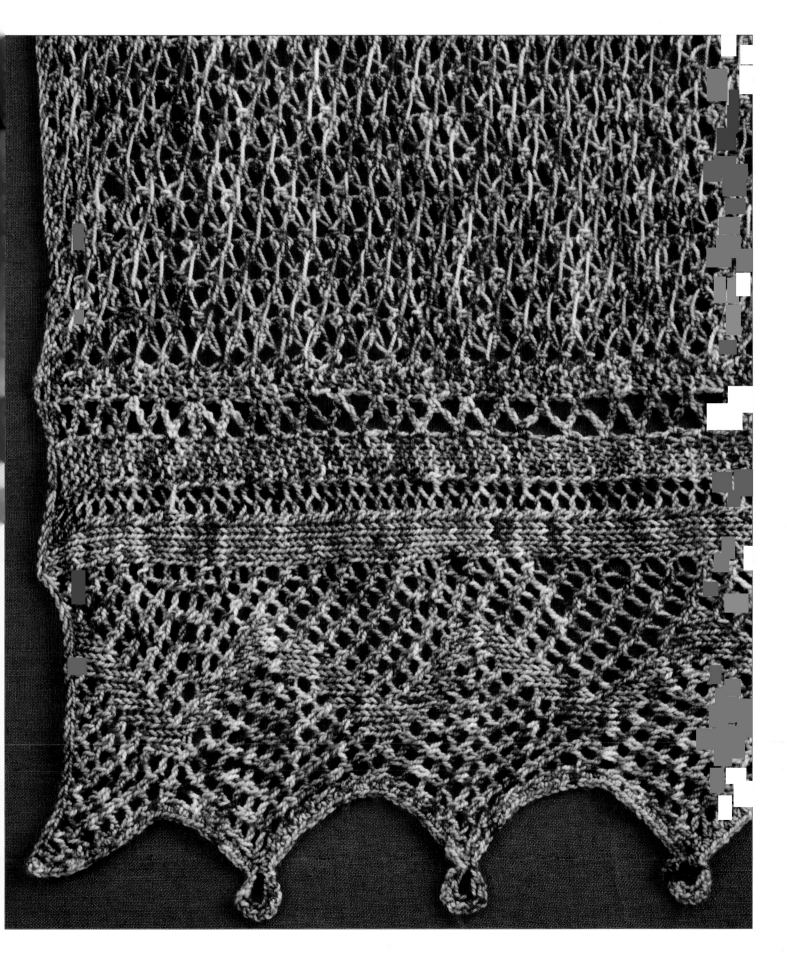

Starfish

DIVIDE FOR ARMHOLES

Next row (RS) Work in pat as established over next 123 sts, k3, join a 2nd ball of yarn, k3, work 6-st rep 10 (11, 12) times across, k2tog, k2, join a 3rd ball of yarn, k2, M1, work in pat to end.

Next row (WS) With 1st ball of yarn, work in pat to last 3 sts, k3, with 2nd ball of yarn, k3, work in pat to last 3 sts, k3, with last ball of yarn, k3, work to end of row. Cont in this manner until armhole measures 8 (8½, 9)"/20.5 (21.5, 23)cm, end with a RS row.

JOIN FOR NECK

Next row (WS) With 1st ball of yarn, work in pat to last 3 sts, k1, k2tog, with 2nd ball of yarn, k1, M1, k2, work in pat to end, with last ball of yarn, work in pat to end.

Next (joining) row (RS) With one ball of yarn only, work in chart pat as established over all sts. Cont in pat until piece measures 19 (19½, 20)"/48 (49.5, 51)cm from beg. Bind off loosely.

SLEEVES

Cast on 49 sts, loosely. Knit 2 rows.

BEGIN CHART 1

Row 1 (RS) Work to rep line, work 6-st rep 6 times across, work to end of chart. Cont to work chart in this manner until row 4 is complete.

Next (inc) row (RS) Work row 1 of chart as established, inc 1 st each side—2 sts inc'd. Cont to rep rows 1–4 and inc 1 st each side every 6th row 0 (4, 8) times more, then every 8th row 11 (9, 7) times, working inc'd sts in garter st (k every row)—73 (77, 81) sts.

Work even in pat until sleeve measures 16 (17, 18)"/40.5 (43, 45.5)cm from beg. Bind off loosely.

BORDERS (MAKE 2)

Cast on 28 sts. Work foll chart 2 pat and work rows 1–28 four times, then rep rows 1–12 (1–14, 1–18) once more. Bind off. With crochet hook and right sides facing, join yarn with sl stitch to first st of straight edge of border (beg RS rows), ch 3, sc in first edge st of side edge of shawl, *ch 3, skip 1 st in edge of border, sc in edge of border, ch 3, skip 1 st in edge of shawl, sc in edge of shawl; rep from * until entire edge is joined. Fasten off.

Sc evenly along edge of border from crochet join, working 2 sc in each yo along shaped edge of border, and working (sc, ch 8, sc) in each point. When entire edge of border has been worked to opposite side of crochet join, fasten off. Rejoin yarn to 1 ch-8 loop, work 1 row of sc into each chain of loop. Fasten off. Repeat in each ch-8 loop. Work other border in same manner.

FINISHING

BLOCKING

Wet pieces and pin to measurements. Allow to dry.

ASSEMBLY

Sew sleeves into armholes. Sew sleeve seams.◈

CHART 1

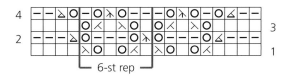

6-st rep

CHART 2

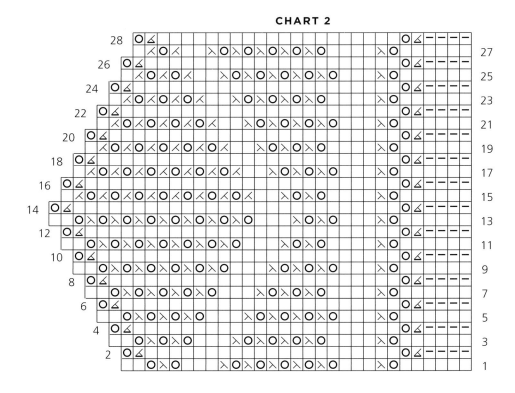

STITCH KEY

- ☐ k on RS, p on WS
- — p on RS, k on WS
- ╱ k2tog on RS
- ◿ k2tog on WS
- ╲ SKP on RS
- ◺ SKP on WS
- O yo
- ⅄ SK2P

Patch of Berries

The allover nubby texture and bright colorway make this shawlette a delicious treat to knit.

MEASUREMENTS (after blocking)
◆ Width along upper edge 37"/94cm
◆ Length excluding crochet trim 18"/45.5cm

MATERIALS
◆ One 1¾oz/50g skein (each 175yd/161m) of Koigu *KPPPM* (merino wool) in #P111

◆ Size 3 (3.25mm) circular needle, 24"/60cm long (used to work back and forth), *or size to obtain gauge*

◆ Size D/3 (3.25mm) crochet hook

◆ 2 stitch markers

GAUGE
28 stitches and 36 rows = 4"/10cm over St st after blocking using size 3 (3.25mm) needle. TAKE TIME TO CHECK GAUGE.

STITCH GLOSSARY
3-st berry Yo, k3, pass first st over last 2 sts.

SHAWL
Cast on 7 sts. Knit 1 row, purl 1 row.
Next (inc) row (RS) K1, yo, k2, yo, place marker (pm), k1 (center st), yo, k2, yo, pm, k1—11 sts.
Purl 1 row.

BEGIN PATTERN STITCH
Row 1 (RS) K1, [yo, k1, work 3-st berry to marker, yo, sl marker, k1] twice—4 sts inc'd.
Row 2 and all WS rows Purl, slipping markers.
Row 3 K1, [yo, k2, work 3-st berry to 1 st before marker, k1, yo, sl marker, k1] twice—4 sts inc'd.
Row 5 K1, [yo, k3, work 3-st berry to 2 sts before marker, k2, yo, sl marker, k1] twice—4 sts inc'd.

Row 6 Purl.
Rep rows 1–6 until 100 rows have been worked from beg—207 sts. Bind off, but do not break yarn.

FINISHING
CROCHET TRIM
With crochet hook, work sc around entire edge of shawl.
Next row Ch 1, *(sc, ch 1, sc) in next sc, sc in next sc; rep from * along entire lower edge of shawl.
Fasten off.

BLOCKING
Wet shawl and pin to measurements, being sure that center spine is straight. Allow to dry.◈

DESIGNED BY MAIE LANDRA
●●●○

Charlotte's Daughter Joy

Though similar in design to the Nellie shawl, Joy has a personality all her own with a variation on the lace pattern and a sunny color palette.

MEASUREMENTS (after blocking)
◆ Width 47"/119.5cm
◆ Length from back neck to center point 23"/58.5cm

MATERIALS
◆ One 1¾oz/50g skein (each 175yd/161m) of Koigu *KPPPM* (merino wool) each in #P118B (A), #P116L (B), #P106L (C), #P632 (D), and #P812X (E) ❶

◆ Size 3 (3.25mm) circular needle, 40"/100cm long (used to work back and forth), *or size to obtain gauge*

◆ Size D/3 (3.25mm) crochet hook

◆ 2 stitch markers

GAUGE
24 stitches and 34 rows = 4"/10cm over lace pattern after blocking using size 3 (3.25mm) needle.
TAKE TIME TO CHECK GAUGE.

STRIPE PATTERN
2 rows A, 2 rows B, 2 rows A, 16 rows B.
[2 rows C, 2 rows B] twice, 24 rows C.
[2 rows D, 2 rows C] twice, 16 rows D.
[2 rows E, 2 rows D] twice, 16 rows E.
[2 rows B, 2 rows E] twice, 8 rows B,
2 rows A.

NOTE
Shawl is worked from the center of the neck to the lower point.

SHAWL
With A, cast on 7 sts.
Knit 1 row, purl 1 row.
Next (inc) row (RS) Sl 1, k1, yo, k1, yo, place marker (pm), k1 (center st), pm, yo, k1, yo, k2—11 sts.
Next row (WS) Sl 1, p to end, slipping markers.
Next (inc) row (RS) Sl 1, k1, yo, knit to marker, yo, sl marker, k1, sl marker, yo, knit to last 2 sts, yo, k2—4 sts inc'd.
Next row Sl 1, p to end.
Rep last 2 rows 5 times more—35 sts.

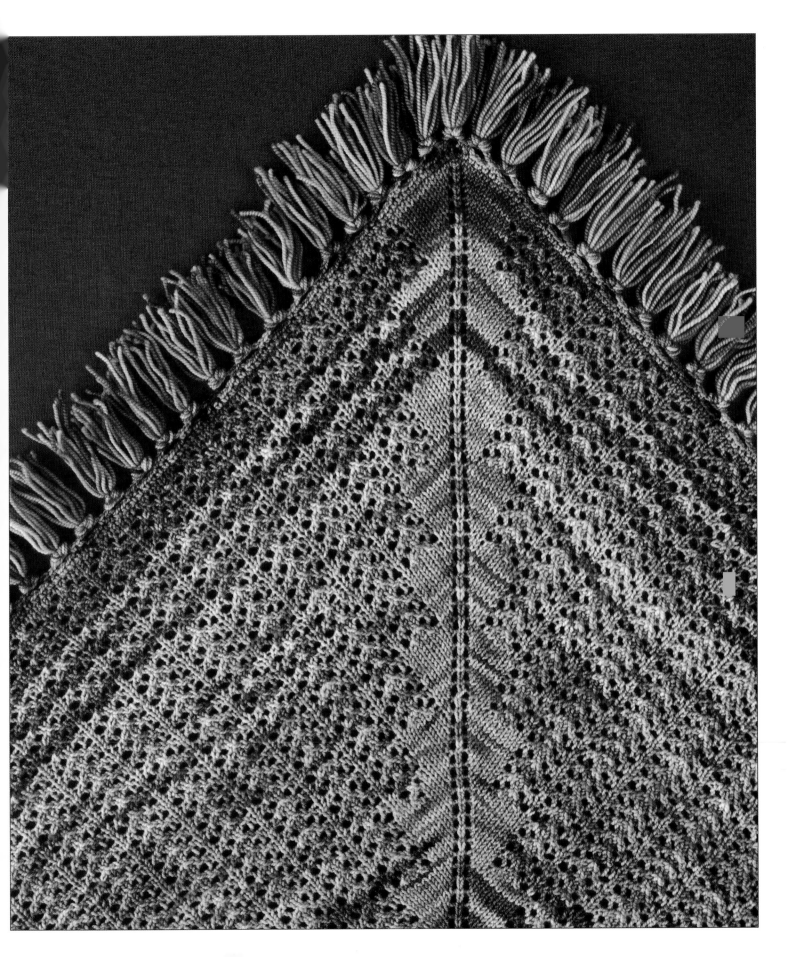

Charlotte's Daughter Joy

BEGIN STRIPE PAT AND CHART

Row 1 With A, sl 1, k1, work row 1 of chart to rep line, work 6-st rep twice, work to end of chart, sl marker, k1, sl marker, work row 1 of chart to rep line, work 6-st rep twice, work to end of chart, k2—4 sts inc'd.

Row 2 Sl 1, p1, work row 2 of chart to rep line, work 6-st rep twice, work to end of chart, sl marker, k1, sl marker, work row 2 of chart to rep line, work 6-st rep twice, work to end of chart, p2.

Cont to work chart in this way, changing colors for stripe pat, until row 12 is complete.

Cont in stripe pat as foll:

Next row (RS) Sl 1, k1, work row 1 of chart to rep line, work 6-st rep 4 times across, work to end of chart, sl marker, k1, work row 1 of chart to rep line, work 6-st rep 4 times across, work to end of chart, k2—4 sts inc'd.

Cont in this way, working 6-st rep twice more on each side of center st for every

12-row rep, until stripe pat is complete (see chart rows 13–20). Bind off loosely.

FINISHING

CROCHET EDGING

With A and crochet hook, work 1 row of sc along entire edge of shawl.

Work evenly along edge as foll:

Next row *Ch 4, sc in next sc; rep from * to end. Fasten off.

BLOCKING

Soak shawl in warm water and pin to maximum size. Allow to dry.

FRINGE

Using colors randomly, cut 4 strands of yarn 3"/7.5cm long. Holding 4 strands tog, fold in half and with crochet hook, draw loop through 1 ch-4 space on lower edge of shawl. Draw ends of strands through folded loop and pull to tighten. Rep in each ch-4 sp along lower edge of shawl.◆

STITCH KEY

☐	k on RS, p on WS
◯	yo
╱	k2tog
╲	SKP
⋏	S2KP

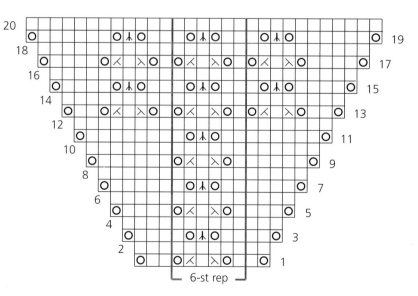

6-st rep

Allusion

DESIGNED BY LORI STEINBERG
●●●○

This cape is a study in contrasting textures and colors, with a swingy fan border adding even more visual interest.

MEASUREMENTS
◆ Width at lower edge approx 62"/157.5cm
◆ Length 19"/48cm

MATERIALS
◆ Two 1¾oz/50g skeins (each 175yd/161m) of Koigu *KPM* (merino wool) in #2400 (A) 🌕①

◆ One 1¾oz/50g skein (each 175yd/161m) of Koigu *KPPPM* (merino wool) each in #P801 (B), #P511 (C), and #460B (D) 🌕①

◆ Size 4 (3.5mm) circular needle, 29"/74cm long (used to work back and forth), *or size to obtain gauge*

◆ One size 4 (3.5mm) double-pointed needle (dpn) for fan border

◆ Stitch markers

GAUGE
26 stitches and 45 rows = 4"/10cm over herringbone pattern after blocking using size 4 (3.5mm) needles.
TAKE TIME TO CHECK GAUGE.

STITCH GLOSSARY
LI (lifted increase) Place RH needle behind LH needle and insert point from top to bottom into the purled top of the st in the row below the next st, knit, then knit the st above it.

HERRINGBONE PATTERN
(multiple of 7 sts plus 1)
Rows 1 and 3 (WS) Purl.
Row 2 *K2tog, k2, LI, k2; rep from * to last st, k1.
Row 4 K1, *k2, LI, k2, k2tog; rep from * to end.
Rep rows 1–4 for herringbone pat.

Allusion

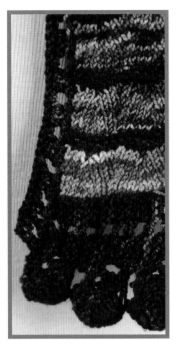

COLOR SEQUENCE FOR HERRINGBONE BANDS
[B, C, D] 3 times, B, C.

FAN BORDER
(beg and end with 13 sts)
Note that each yo counts as a stitch.
Row 1 (RS) K7, k2tog, (yo) twice, k2tog, k1, k2tog (1 border st with 1 shawl st).
Row 2 Sl 1, k2, p1, k9.
Row 3 K to last st, k2tog.
Row 4 Sl 1, k to end.
Row 5 K2, [(yo) twice, k1] 3 times, (yo) twice, k2, k2tog, (yo) twice, k2tog, k1, k2tog—21 sts.
Row 6 Sl 1, k2, p1, k4, [p1, k2] 3 times, p1, k3.
Rows 7 and 8 Rep rows 3 and 4.
Row 9 K15, k2tog, (yo) twice, k2tog, k1, k2tog.
Row 10 Sl 1, k2, p1, k5, (yo) 3 times, k12 wrapping 3 times for each st.
Row 11 Sl 12 to RH needle, dropping extra wraps, sl these 12 sts back to LH needle and k12tog, return st to LH needle and k it again, k1, p1, k1, k8, k2tog—13 sts.
Row 12 Sl 1, k to end.
Rep rows 1–12 for fan border.

NOTES
1. Shawl is worked from the neck edge down.
2. Cut yarn at the end of each color band. Do not carry up the side.

SHAWL
With A, cast on 71 sts. Knit 4 rows.
Next (inc) row (RS) Knit, inc 14 sts evenly across—85 sts.

BEGIN COLOR AND PATTERN SEQUENCE
With B, work 8 rows in herringbone pat.
Next row (WS) Purl.
*****Next row** With A, knit, inc 14 sts evenly across—99 sts.
Knit 4 rows more.
Next row (RS) Knit, inc 14 sts evenly across—113 sts.
With C, work 8 rows in herringbone pat.
Next row (WS) Purl.
Cont in color sequence as established, rep from * until color sequence is complete—365 sts.
Next row (RS) With A, knit, inc 1 st—366 sts. Cut A.

FAN BORDER
With dpn and A, cast on 13 sts.
Next row (WS) K13.
Work in fan border pat, attaching as directed at end of every RS row. Rep rows 1–12 of fan border pat until all shawl sts have been joined. Bind off.

FINISHING
With RS facing, circular needle and A, beg at top left corner, pick up and k 96 sts along left edge to just above fan.
Next row (WS) Knit.
Next row *K2tog, (yo) twice, SKP; rep from * to end.
Next row Knit, working k1, p1 in each double yarn over.
Next row Knit. Bind off. Rep for other side.

BLOCKING
Pin to measurements and semicircle shape. Pin each fan. Spray with water and allow to dry. ❖

Groovy

DESIGNED BY MAIE LANDRA
● ● ● ○

Stay cool and casual from spring through fall with an airy drop-stitch pattern, long fringe, and a bright palette.

MEASUREMENTS (after blocking)
◆ Width 15"/38cm
◆ Length 75"/190.5cm

MATERIALS
◆ Five 1¾oz/50g skeins (each 175yd/161m) of Koigu KPPPM (merino wool) in #P150

◆ Size 6 (4mm) circular needle, 60"/152.4cm long (used to work back and forth), or size to obtain gauge

GAUGE
16 stitches and 16 rows = 4"/10cm over drop stitch pattern after blocking using size 6 (4mm) needle.
TAKE TIME TO CHECK GAUGE.

DROP STITCH PATTERN
(over any number of sts)
Rows 1 and 2 Knit tbl.
Row 3 (RS) K2tbl, *[yo] five times, k1tbl; rep from * to last 2 sts, [yo] 5 times, k2tbl.
Row 4 K2tbl, *drop 5 yos, k1tbl; rep from * to last 2 sts, drop 5 yos, k2tbl.
Rep rows 1–4 for drop st pat.

NOTES
1. All sts are knit through the back loop.
2. Leave a loop 16"/40.5cm long at the beg and end of every row to form the fringe on the sides.

SHAWL
Cast on 300 sts, leaving a 16"/40.5cm tail.
Next 2 rows Knit tbl.
Leaving a loop 16"/40.5cm long at the beg and end of every row, rep rows 1–6 of drop st pat 10 times.
Next 4 rows Knit tbl.
Bind off.

FINISHING
BLOCKING
Place shawl flat on a towel and pin to measurements, being sure that stitches are straight. Spray with water, allow to dry.

FRINGE
Tie each group of tails tog close to the edge of the garter st sections. Cut loops to separate fringe. ◈

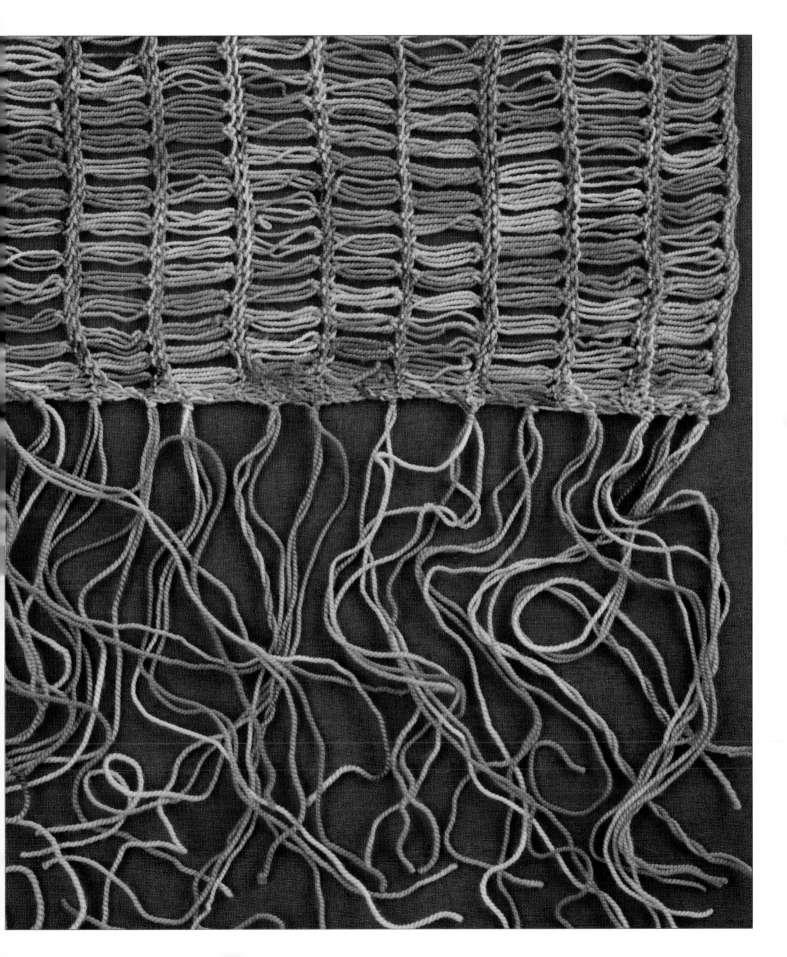

Waves

With a wave stitch pattern that ebbs and flows throughout, this rectangular wrap is a go-to cover-up for breezy days at the beach.

MEASUREMENTS
◆ Width 21"/53.5cm
◆ Length 54"/137cm excluding edging

MATERIALS
◆ Five 1¾oz/50g skeins (each 114yd/104m) of Koigu *Kersti Merino Crepe* (merino wool) in #K439 (A) 🔳

◆ 4 skeins in #K463 (B)

◆ One pair size 6 (4mm) needles *or size to obtain gauge*

◆ Size E/4 (3.5mm) crochet hook

GAUGE
18 stitches and 32 rows = 4"/10cm over wave pattern using size 6 (4mm) needles.
TAKE TIME TO CHECK GAUGE.

EDGE PATTERN
(over an even number of sts)
Rows 1 and 2 With B, knit.
Row 3 (RS) With A, *k1, [yo] twice; rep from * to last st, end k1.
Row 4 With A, knit, dropping all yos off needle.
Rows 5 and 6 With B, knit.
Rows 7 and 8 Rep rows 3 and 4.
Rows 9 and 10 With B, knit.

Waves

WAVE PATTERN
(multiple of 10 sts plus 6)
Rows 1 and 2 With B, knit.
Row 3 (RS) With A, k6, *[yo] once, k1, [yo] twice, k1, [yo] 3 times, k1, [yo] twice, k1, [yo] once, k6; rep from * to end.
Row 4 With A, knit, dropping all yos off needle.
Rows 5 and 6 With B, knit.
Row 7 With A, k1, *[yo] once, k1, [yo] twice, k1, [yo] 3 times, k1, [yo] twice, k1, [yo] once, k6; rep from *, end last rep k1.
Row 8 With A, rep row 4.
Rep rows 1–8 for wave pat.

WRAP
With B, cast on 96 sts.
Work 10 rows in edge pat.
Place markers at each end of row.
Work in wave pat until piece measures 52"/132cm from beg, end with a pat row 2.
Place markers at each end of row.
Work 10 rows in edge pat.
With B, bind off. Cut yarn.

FINISHING
CROCHET EDGING
With crochet hook and A, work along cast-on edge as foll:
Join yarn to one corner of wrap, sc along edge to first marker, *ch 15, turn and sc into each ch, 8 sc along edge; rep from * to last marker, ch 15, turn and sc into each ch, sc along edge to end. Fasten off. Rep along bound-off edge. Remove markers.

Join yarn to end of wrap and ch 1. Working evenly into edge, sc 12, ch 15, work 1 sc in each ch, work *8 sc, ch 15, work 1 sc in each ch; rep from *, end working 12 sc in last section of wrap.
Fasten off. Rep along 2nd long edge of wrap. ◈

Tumble Leaves

Leaf lace on the body, a dramatic border, and a rich jewel-tone colorway add up to the perfect accessory for a chilly autumn day.

MEASUREMENTS
◆ Width including border, after blocking 92"/233.5cm
◆ Length 23½"/60cm

MATERIALS
◆ Seven 1¾oz/50g skeins (each 175yd/160m) of Koigu *KPPPM* (merino wool) in #P623 **1**

◆ One pair size 6 (4mm) needles *or size to obtain gauge*

GAUGE
19 stitches and 18 rows = 4"/10cm over leaf pattern after blocking using size 6 (4mm) needles.
TAKE TIME TO CHECK GAUGE.

LEAF PATTERN
(multiple of 16 sts)
Row 1 (RS) P1, yo, k3, yo, SK2P, yo, k2tog, yo, k2, SK2P, k2, yo.
Row 2 and all WS rows Purl.
Row 3 P1, yo, k5, yo, SK2P, yo, k2, SK2P, k2, yo.
Row 5 P1, yo, k2, SK2P, k2, yo, SKP, yo, k1, SK2P, k1, yo, k1, yo.
Row 7 P1, yo, k2, SK2P, k2, yo, SKP, yo, S2KP, yo, k3, yo.
Row 9 P1, yo, k2, SK2P, k2, yo, SK2P, yo, k5, yo.
Row 11 P1, [yo, k1] twice, SK2P, k1, yo, k2tog, yo, k2, SK2P, k2, yo.
Row 12 Purl.
Rep rows 1–12 for leaf pat.

BORDER PATTERN
(begin with 20 sts, st count changes when working pat)
Row 1 (RS) K2, yo, k2, SKP, k4, k2tog, k2, yo, k1, [yo, SKP] twice, yo, k1.
Row 2 and all WS rows Purl.
Row 3 K3, yo, k2, SKP, k2, k2tog, k2, yo, k3, [yo, SKP] twice, yo, k1.
Row 5 K2, yo, SKP, yo, k2, SKP, k2tog, k2, yo, k5, [yo, SKP] twice, yo, k1.

Tumble Leaves

Row 7 K3, yo, SKP, yo, k2, SKP, k4, k2tog, k2, yo, k1, [yo, SKP] twice, yo, k1.
Row 9 K2, [yo, SKP] twice, yo, k2, SKP, k2, k2tog, k2, yo, k3, [yo, SKP] twice, yo, k1.
Row 11 K3, [yo, SKP] twice, yo, k2, SKP, k2tog, k2, yo, k5, [yo, SKP] twice, yo, k1.
Row 13 K2, [yo, SKP] 3 times, yo, k2, SKP, k4, k2tog, k2, yo, k1, [yo, SKP] twice, yo, k1.
Row 15 K3, [yo, SKP] 3 times, yo, k2, SKP, k2, k2tog, k2, yo, k3, [yo, SKP] twice, yo, k1.
Row 17 K4, [yo, SKP] 3 times, yo, k2, SKP, k2tog, k2, yo, k5, [yo, SKP] twice, yo, k1.
Row 19 K2tog, k2, [yo, k2tog] 3 times, yo, k1, yo, k2, SKP, k4, k2tog, k2, [yo, k2tog] 3 times.
Row 21 K3, [k2tog, yo] 3 times, k3, yo, k2, SKP, k2, k2tog, k2, [yo, k2tog] 3 times.
Row 23 K2, [k2tog, yo] 3 times, k5, yo, k2, SKP, k2tog, k2, [yo, k2tog] 3 times.
Row 25 K1, [k2tog, yo] 3 times, k1, yo, k2, SKP, k4, k2tog, k2, [yo, k2tog] 3 times.
Row 27 K2, [k2tog, yo] twice, k3, yo, k2, SKP, k2, k2tog, k2, [yo, k2tog] 3 times.
Row 29 K1, [k2tog, yo] twice, k5, yo, k2, SKP, k2tog, k2, [yo, k2tog] 3 times.
Row 31 K2, k2tog, yo, k1, yo, k2, SKP, k4, k2tog, k2, [yo, k2tog] 3 times.
Row 33 K1, k2tog, yo, k3, yo, k2, SKP, k2, k2tog, k2, [yo, k2tog] 3 times.
Row 35 K7, yo, k2, SKP, k2tog, k2, [yo, k2tog] 3 times.
Row 36 Purl.
Rep rows 1–36 for border lace pat.

NOTE
Lace patterns may be worked from text or chart.

SHAWL
Cast on 113 sts.

BEGIN LEAF PAT OR CHART
Row 1 (RS) Work row 1 of 16-st rep of leaf pat 7 times across, p1.
Row 2 P1, work next row of 16-st rep of leaf pat 7 times across.
Cont to work pat in this way until row 12 is complete. Rep rows 1–12 until piece measures approx 76"/193cm from beg. Bind off.

FINISHING
BORDER (MAKE 2)
Cast on 20 sts.
Begin border pat or chart.
Work rows 1–36 of border pat 3 times.
Bind off.
Sew border pieces to cast-on and bound-off edges of shawl.

BLOCKING
Soak shawl in warm water, pin flat, shaping to maximum size.
Allow to dry.◈

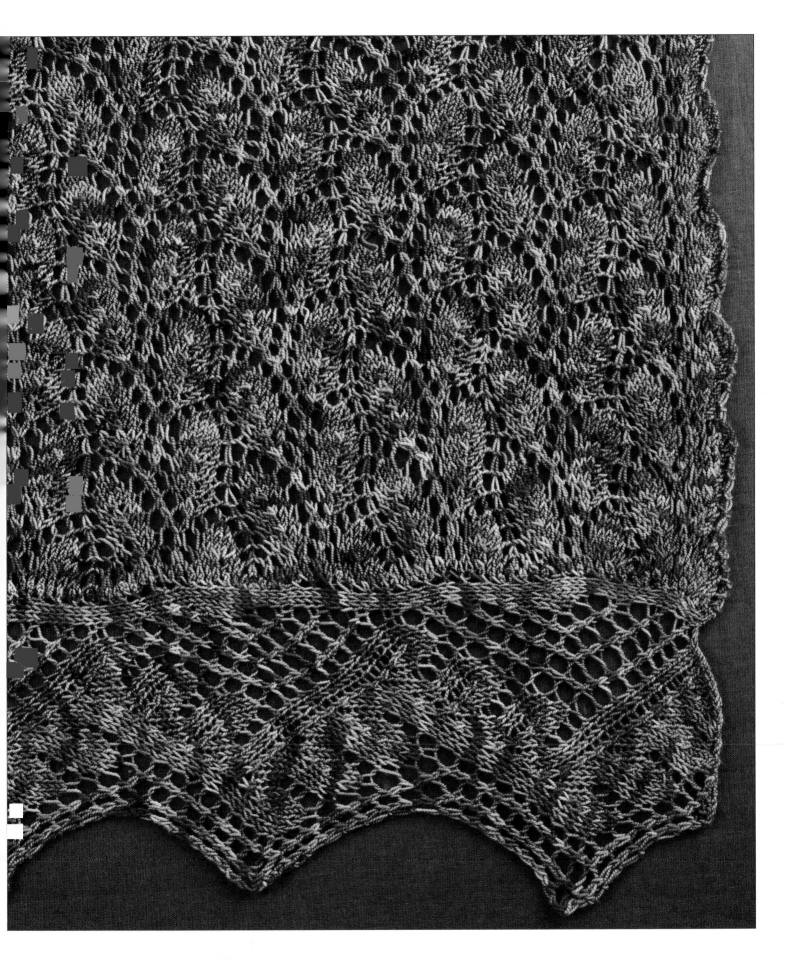

Tumble Leaves

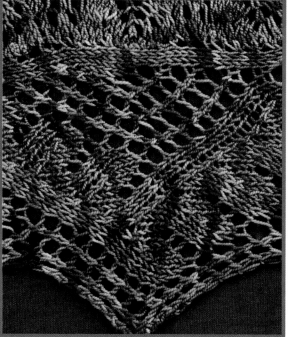

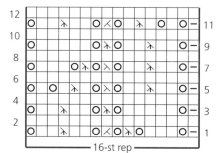

beg with 20 sts

LEAF CHART

16-st rep

STITCH KEY

□	k on RS, p on WS
−	p on RS, k on WS
╱	k2tog
╲	SKP
○	yo
⋏	SK2P

Dash

A simple, customizable stripe sequence using seven colorways makes each finished version of this shawl a unique work of art.

MEASUREMENTS (after blocking)
◆ Width 68"/172.5cm
◆ Length 36"/91.5cm

MATERIALS
◆ One 1¾oz/50g skein (each 114yd/104m) of Koigu *Kersti Merino Crepe* (merino wool) each in #P121, #P100L, #P506A, #P130, #P151, #P620, #K334, and #P127 ③

◆ Size 6 (4mm) circular needle, 60"/152.4cm long (used to work back and forth), *or size to obtain gauge*

◆ Size E/4 (3.5mm) crochet hook

◆ 2 stitch markers

GAUGE
16 stitches and 29 rows = 4"/10cm over dash pat after blocking using size 6 (4mm) needle.
TAKE TIME TO CHECK GAUGE.

STITCH GLOSSARY
LI (lifted increase) K into the st below the next st on LH needle without dropping st from LH needle, k the next st, dropping both sts from LH needle.

DASH PATTERN
(multiple of 10 sts plus 6)
Row 1 (RS) P6, *k4, p6; rep from * to end.
Row 2 and all WS rows Purl.
Rows 3 and 7 Knit.
Row 5 P1, *k4, p6; rep from * to last 5 sts, k4, p1.
Row 8 Purl.
Rep rows 1–8 for dash pat.

COLOR SEQUENCE
Using the 7 colors randomly for 2 stripes each, work 12 rows in each color until 10 stripes (not counting the first color) have been worked, then work 8 rows in each color to the end.

Dash

SHAWL

With first color, cast on 7 sts. Knit 1 row, purl 1 row.

Next (inc) row (RS) Sl 1, [LI] twice, place marker (pm), k1, pm, [LI] twice, k1—11 sts.

Next row Sl 1, p to marker, sl marker, k1, sl marker, p to end.

Next (inc) row (RS) Sl 1, LI, k to 1 st before marker, LI, sl marker, p1, sl marker, LI, k to last 2 sts, LI, k1—4 sts inc'd.

Rep last 2 rows twice more—23 sts.

Next row Sl 1, p to marker, sl marker, k1, sl marker, p to end.

SET UP DASH PATTERN

Set-up row 1 (RS) Sl 1, LI, k1, p6, k1, LI, sl marker, p1, sl marker, LI, k1, p6, k1, LI, k1—4 sts inc'd.

Set-up row 2 Sl 1, p to marker, sl marker, k1, sl marker, p to end.

Set-up row 3 Sl 1, LI, k to 1 st before marker, LI, sl marker, p1, sl marker, LI, k to last 2 sts, LI, k1—4 sts inc'd.

Set-up row 4 Rep set-up row 2.

Set-up row 5 (RS) Sl 1, LI, p6, k4, p2, LI, sl marker, p1, sl marker, LI, p2, k4, p6, LI, k1—35 sts.

Set-up rows 6–8 Rep set-up rows 2–4—39 sts.

Set-up row 9 (RS) Sl 1, LI, k2, p6, k4, p4, LI, sl marker, p1, sl marker, LI, p4, k4, p6, k2, LI, k1—4 sts inc'd.

Rep set-up rows 2–4 once more—47 sts.

BEGIN DASH PATTERN

Note Work incs into dash pat.

Next row (RS) Sl 1, LI, work from * of row 1 of dash pat to 1 st before marker, LI, sl marker, p1, sl marker, LI, work from * of row 1 of dash pat to last 2 sts, LI, k1.

Next row Sl 1, work row 2 of dash pat to marker, sl marker, k1, sl marker, work row 2 of dash pat to end.

Cont in this manner, working incs on RS rows, until row 8 is complete—63 sts. Change to 2nd color.

Cont to inc and work pat as established, rep rows 1–8 of dash pat, working color sequence until last color has been used twice.

FINISHING

CROCHET EDGING

Work 1 row of sc along side edges of shawl.

BLOCKING

Wet shawl and pin to measurements. Allow to dry.

FRINGE

Cut 4 strands of yarn 10"/25.5cm long. Holding 4 strands tog, fold in half and with crochet hook, draw folded loop through sc at center point of shawl. Draw ends of strands through loop and pull to tighten. Rep in approx every 5th sc along lower edge of shawl.◈

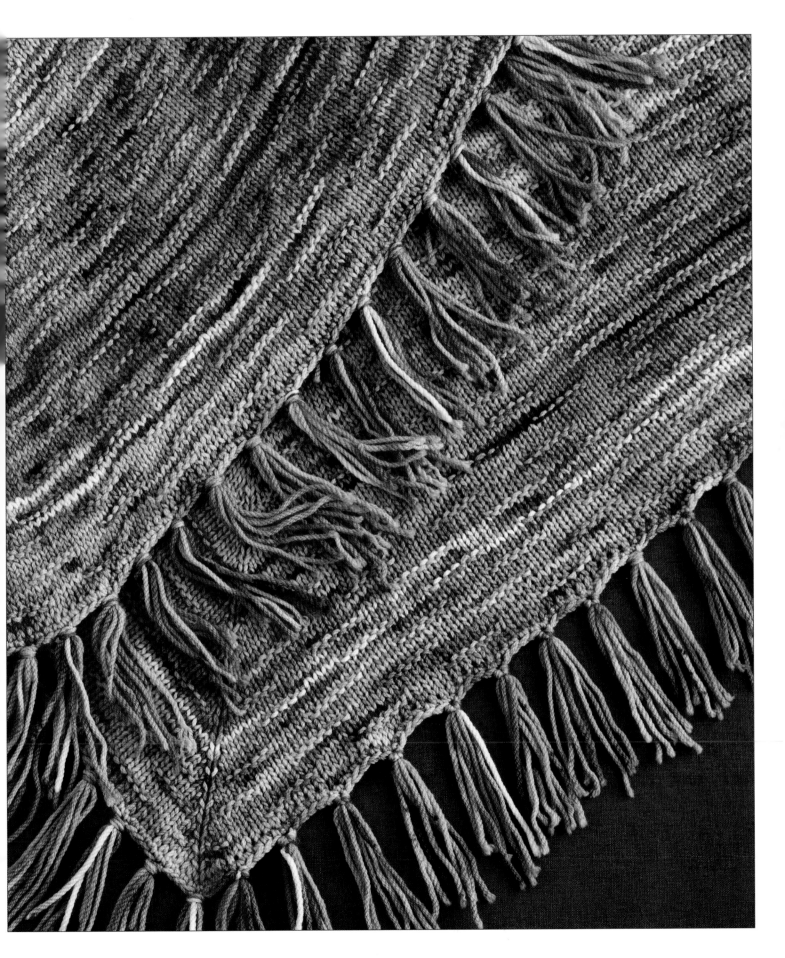

Lucky Lady

The garter stitch center of this square shawl is set within a border of horseshoe lace, perhaps bringing a bit of luck to those who wear it.

MEASUREMENTS (after blocking)
◆ Approximately
42 x 42"/106.5 x 106.5cm

MATERIALS
◆ Six 1¾oz/50g skeins
(each 185yd/168m) of Koigu *Mori*
(wool/mulberry silk) in #M475 **(1)**

◆ Size 9 (5.5mm) circular needle,
40"/101.5cm long (used to work back and forth), *or size to obtain gauge*

◆ Stitch markers

GAUGE
16 stitches and 32 rows = 4"/10cm
over garter stitch after blocking using
size 9 (5.5mm) needle.
TAKE TIME TO CHECK GAUGE.

STITCH GLOSSARY
kfbf Knit into front, back, front of next st to inc 2 sts.

NOTES
1. The garter stitch square body of the shawl is worked back and forth in rows.
2. The lace border is picked up and knit along the edge of the square, then worked in rounds.

SHAWL
Cast on 1 st.
Next row Kfb—2 sts.
Next (inc) row (RS) Sl 1 purlwise wyif, kfb, k to end—1 st inc'd.

Rep inc row every row until there are 128 sts on needle.
Next row Sl 1 purlwise wyif, k to end.
Next (dec) row Sl 1 purlwise wyif, ssk, k to end—1 st dec'd.
Rep dec row every row until 1 st rem.
Fasten off.

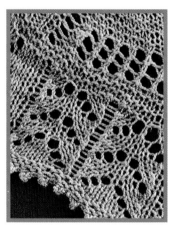

Lucky Lady

BORDERS

With RS facing, beg in first st after corner, [pick up and k 64 sts along edge to next corner, place marker (pm), pick up and k 1 st in corner, pm] 4 times around. Join to work in the round.

Next rnd [P64, sl marker, M1, k1, M1, sl marker] 4 times around—3 sts each corner.

Rnd 1 [*K2tog, yo; rep from * to next marker, sl marker, k1, yo, k to 1 st before next marker, yo, k1, sl marker] 4 times around—5 sts each corner.

Rnd 2 Purl.

Rnd 3 [*Yo, k2tog; rep from * to next marker, sl marker, k1, yo, k to 1 st before next marker, yo, k1, sl marker] 4 times around—7 sts each corner.

Rnd 4 Purl.

Rep rnds 1 and 2 once more—9 sts each corner.

Rnd 7 [K to marker, sl marker, k1, yo, k to 1 st before next marker, yo, k1] 4 times around—11 sts each corner.

Rnd 8 Purl.

Rep rnds 7 and 8 once more, then rnd 7 once.

Next rnd Purl, dec 1 st in each edge—63 sts each edge, 15 sts each corner.

BEGIN CHART 1

Rnd 1 [K2, work 10-st rep 6 times across, k1, sl marker, k1, yo, k to 1 st before marker, yo, k1, sl marker] 4 times around—17 sts each corner.

Cont to work chart in this way until rnd 8 is complete. Rep rnds 1–8 twice more—39 sts each corner.

Purl 1 rnd.

Next rnd [K to marker, sl marker, k1, yo, k to 1 st before next marker, yo, k1] 4 times around—41 sts each corner.

Purl 1 rnd.

Next (inc) rnd [K5, (kfbf) 3 times, *k7, (kfbf) 3 times; rep from * to last 5 sts, k5, sl marker, k1, yo, k to 1 st before marker, yo, k1, sl marker] 4 times around—99 sts for each edge, 43 sts for each corner.

Next rnd Purl, removing markers and placing new markers on each side of center st of each corner.

BEGIN CHARTS 2 AND 3

Rnd 1 [K2, work 16-st rep of chart 2 six times across, k1, work rnd 1 of chart 3 to rep line, work 9-st rep twice, work to next rep line, work 9-st rep twice, work to end of chart 3].

Cont to work in this manner until rnd 6 of chart 2 is complete. Rep rnds 1–6 of chart 2, until rnd 18 of chart 3 is complete—160 sts between markers.

Next rnd [Knit to marker, yo, sl marker, k1, sl marker, yo] 4 times around—162 sts between markers.

Purl 1 rnd.

Rep last 2 rnds twice more—166 sts between markers.

Bind off as foll: *Cast on 2 sts to LH needle, bind off 4 sts, sl rem st to LH needle; rep from * until all sts have been bound off. Fasten off.

FINISHING

BLOCKING

Pin garter st center into a 32"/81cm square. Pin corners, being sure to line up eyelet holes. Pin border edges, pinning out points. Spray and let dry.◈

Lucky Lady

CHART 1

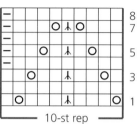

10-st rep

CHART 2

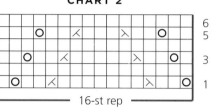

16-st rep

CHART 3

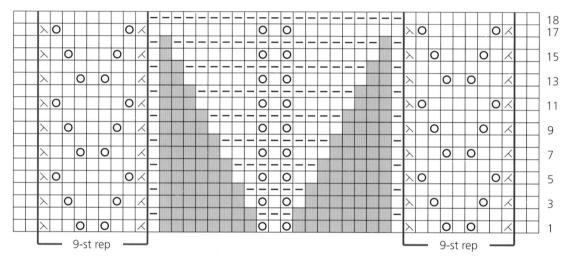

9-st rep   9-st rep

STITCH KEY

☐ k on RS, p on WS

− p on RS, k on WS

╱ k2tog

╲ SKP

⊙ yo

▨ no stitch

⟊ S2KP

Victoria

A bright and punchy colorway puts a fun, modern spin on a traditional lacework design with delicate sewn-on borders.

MEASUREMENTS (after blocking)
◆ Width 24¾"/63cm
◆ Length including borders 83"/210.5cm

MATERIALS
◆ Seven 1¾oz/50g skeins
(each 175yd/161m) of Koigu *Mori*
(mulberry silk/merino wool)
in #M803 **①**

◆ One pair size 3 (3.25mm) needles
or size to obtain gauge

GAUGE
16 stitches and 32 rows = 4"/10cm over chart pattern after blocking using size 3 (3.25mm) needles.
TAKE TIME TO CHECK GAUGE.

NOTE
Borders are worked separately and sewn to shawl in finishing.

SHAWL
Cast on 99 sts. Work 2 rows in St st (k on RS, p on WS).

BEGIN CHART
Row 1 (RS) Work to rep line, work 16-st rep 5 times across, work to end of chart. Cont to work chart in this way until piece measures approx 81"/205.5cm from beg, end with a chart row 6. Knit 1 row. Bind off.

Victoria

BORDERS

(make 2)

Note that the stitch count changes from row to row and each yo counts as a stitch. Cast on 10 sts.

Row 1 (RS) Sl 1, k2, yo, k2tog, [(yo) twice, k2tog] twice, k1—12 sts.

Row 2 K3, [p1, k2] twice, yo, k2tog, k1.

Row 3 Sl 1, k2, yo, k2tog, k2, [(yo) twice, k2tog] twice, k1—14 sts.

Row 4 K3, p1, k2, p1, k4, yo, k2tog, k1.

Row 5 Sl 1, k2, yo, k2tog, k4, [(yo) twice, k2tog] twice, k1—16 sts.

Row 6 K3, p1, k2, p1, k6, yo, k2tog, k1.

Row 7 Sl 1, k2, yo, k2tog, k11.

Row 8 Bind off 6 sts, k until there are 7 sts on RH needle, yo, k2tog, k1.

Rep rows 1–8 for 21 times or until straight edge of border is same length as cast-on edge of shawl, binding off all sts on final row 8.

FINISHING

Sew border strips to cast-on and bound-off edges of shawl.

BLOCKING

Pin to measurements and steam. ◈

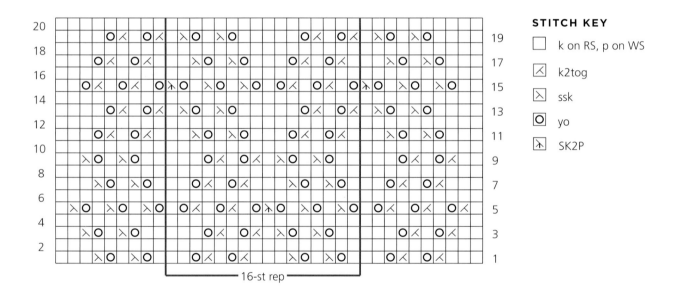

16-st rep

STITCH KEY

☐ k on RS, p on WS

◿ k2tog

◺ ssk

⊙ yo

⋏ SK2P

Stroke of Midnight

DESIGNED BY MAIE LANDRA

●●○○

Meditative lacework in a calming color palette makes for a wrap that is as easy and relaxing to knit as it is to wear.

MEASUREMENTS (after blocking)
◆ Width 82"/208cm
◆ Length 18"/45.5cm

MATERIALS
◆ Ten 1¾oz/50g skeins
(each 175yd/160m) of Koigu *KPPPM*
(merino wool) in P123 (**1**)

◆ Size 3 (3.25mm) circular needle,
40"/100cm long (used to work back and
forth), *or size to obtain gauge*

◆ Size D/3 (3.25mm) crochet hook

GAUGE
28 stitches and 36 rows = 4"/10cm
over St st after blocking using size
3 (3.25mm) needle.
TAKE TIME TO CHECK GAUGE.

LACE PATTERN 1
(over an even number of sts plus 4)
Rows 1–4 (RS) Knit.
Rows 5 and 7 K2, *yo, k2tog;
rep from * to last 2 sts, k2.
Rows 6 and 8 K2, *yo, p2tog;
rep from * to last 2 sts, k2.
Rows 9 and 10 Knit.
Rep rows 1–10 for lace pat 1.

LACE PATTERN 2
(over an even number of sts plus 4)
Rows 1–4 Knit.
Rows 5, 7, and 9 (RS) K2, *yo, k2tog;
rep from * to last 2 sts, k2.
Rows 6, 8, and 10 K2, *yo, p2tog;
rep from * to last 2 sts, k2.
Rows 11 and 12 Knit.
Rep rows 1–12 for lace pat 2.

SHAWL
Cast on 420 sts.

BEGIN LACE PATS
[Work rows 1–10 of lace pat 1 three times,
work rows 1–12 of lace pat 2 three times]
twice.
Rep rows 1–10 of lace pat 1 three times
more. Knit 2 rows. Bind off.

FINISHING
BLOCKING
Wet piece and hang sideways from
bound-off edge, pinning to ensure a
straight edge. Allow to dry. ◈

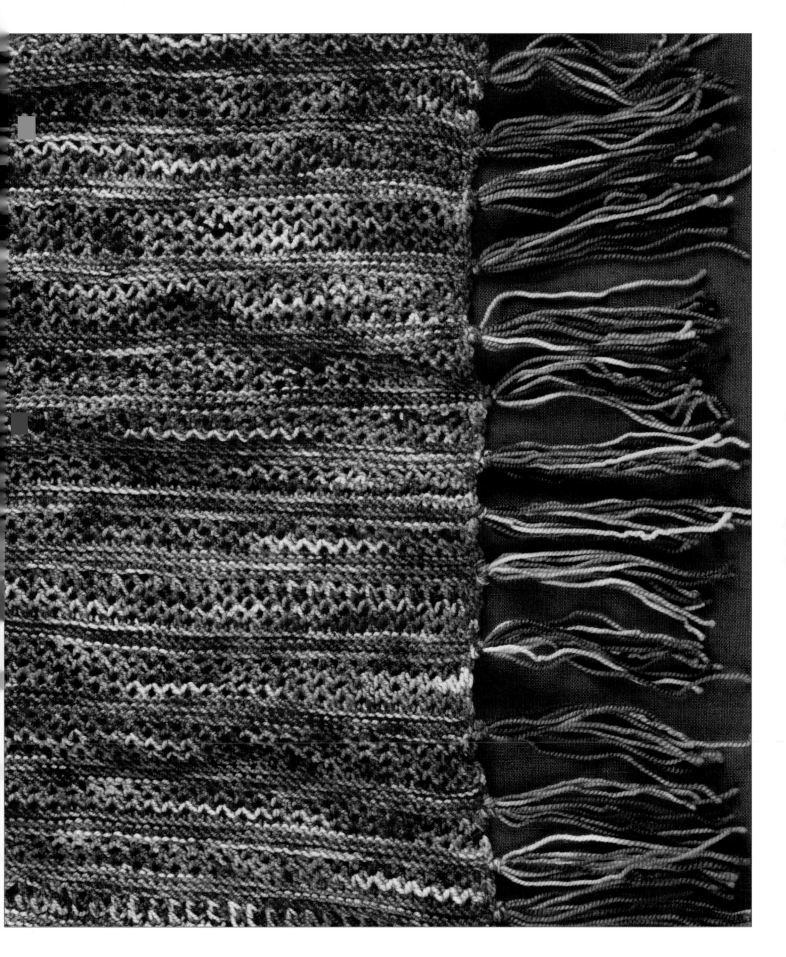

Elizabeth

Pretty pastels in a graceful laceweight are the right combination for a cheery spring wrap.

MEASUREMENTS (after blocking)
◆ Width 24½"/62.5cm
◆ Length 80"/203cm (including border)

MATERIALS
◆ Four 1¾oz/50g skeins (each 292yd/161m) of Koigu *Lace Merino* (merino wool) in #L355 (0)

◆ Size 6 (4mm) needles, 32"/80cm long, *or size to obtain gauge*

GAUGE
20 stitches and 23 rows = 4"/10cm over lace pat after blocking using size 6 (4mm) needles.
TAKE TIME TO CHECK GAUGE.

LACE PATTERN
(multiple of 10 sts plus 11)
Rows 1, 3, 5, and 7 (RS) K1, *yo, k3, SK2P, k3, yo, k1; rep from * to end.
Row 2 and all WS rows Purl.
Rows 9, 11, 13, and 15 K2tog, *k3, yo, k1, yo, k3, SK2P; rep from * to last 9 sts, k3, yo, k1, yo, k3, SKP.
Row 16 Rep row 2.
Rep rows 1–16 for lace pat.

BORDER PATTERN
(multiple of 11 sts)
Row 1 (RS) K2tog, k2tog, [yo, k1] 4 times, yo, SKP, SKP; rep from * to end.
Row 2 Purl.
Rep rows 1 and 2 for border pat.

Elizabeth

NOTES

1. Slip the first st and purl the last st of every row throughout.
2. Lace pattern can be worked using chart or text.
3. Borders are worked separately and sewn on.

SHAWL

Cast on 123 sts.
Knit 2 rows.

BEGIN LACE PAT

Row 1 (RS) Sl 1, work to rep line, work 10-st rep 11 times across, work to end of chart, p1.
Cont to work chart in this manner until row 16 is complete.
Rep rows 1–16 until shawl measures approx 75½"/191.5cm from beg. Bind off.

BORDER (MAKE 2)

Cast on 123 sts.
Next row (RS) Sl 1, k to last st, p1.
Next row Sl 1, p to end.

BEGIN BORDER PAT

Row 1 (RS) Sl 1, work 11-st rep 12 times across, p1.
Next row Sl 1, p to end.
Rep last 2 rows 5 times more.
Next row (RS) Sl 1, k to last st, p1.
Bind off loosely.

FINISHING

Sew bound-off edges of borders to cast-on and bound-off edges of shawl.

BLOCKING

Wet shawl and pin to measurements. Allow to dry.◈

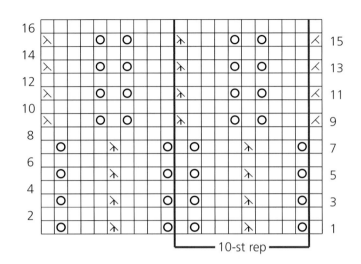

10-st rep

STITCH KEY

k2tog

SKP

yo

SK2P

Maria

This voluminous shawl can be draped in a variety of ways to show off its delicate Estonian lace and braided fringe.

MEASUREMENTS (after blocking)
◆ Width 74"/188cm
◆ Length 41"/104cm

MATERIALS
◆ Eight 1¾oz/50g skeins
(each 175yd/161m) of Koigu *KPPPM*
(merino wool) in P100 (**1**)

◆ Size 4 (3.5mm) circular needle,
40"/100cm long (used to work back and
forth), *or size to obtain gauge*

◆ Size C/2 (2.75mm) crochet hook

◆ 2 stitch markers

GAUGE
16 stitches and 28 rows = 4"/10cm
in lace pat after blocking using
size 4 (3.5mm) needle.
TAKE TIME TO CHECK GAUGE.

NOTE
Each [yo] counts as a stitch.

Maria

SHAWL

Cast on 9 sts.

Next row (RS) K4, place marker (pm), k1, pm, k4.

Next row Sl 1, p1, k to marker, sl marker, p1, sl marker, k to last 2 sts, p2.

Next (inc) row Sl 1, k1, yo, k to marker, yo, sl marker, k1, sl marker, yo, k to last 2 sts, yo, k2—4 sts inc'd.

Next row Sl 1, p1, k to marker, sl marker, p1, sl marker, k to last 2 sts, p2.

Rep last 2 rows 3 times more—25 sts.

BEGIN LACE PAT

Row 1 (RS) Sl 1, k1, yo, k1, *k2tog, [yo] twice, SKP; rep from * to 1 st before marker, k1, yo, sl marker, k1, sl marker, yo, k1, *k2tog, [yo] twice, SKP; rep from * to last 3 sts, k1, yo, k2—4 sts inc'd.

Row 2 and all WS rows Sl 1, p1, k to marker working k1, p1 in each double yo, sl marker, p1, sl marker, k to last 2 sts, p2.

Row 3 Sl 1, k1, yo, k to marker, yo, sl marker, k1, sl marker, yo, k to last 2 sts, yo, k3—4 sts inc'd.

Row 5 Sl 1, k1, yo, k1, *yo, SKP, k2tog, yo; rep from * to 1 st before marker, k1, yo, sl marker, k1, sl marker, yo, k1, *yo, SKP, k2tog, yo; rep from * to last 3 sts, k1, yo, k2—4 sts inc'd.

Row 7 Rep row 3.

Row 8 Rep row 2.

Rep rows 1–8 until piece measures approx 41"/104cm from beg or until 2 skeins rem, end with a WS row. Bind off.

FINISHING

CROCHET EDGING

With crochet hook, join yarn with sl st in upper corner of shawl, sc in same st as sl st, *ch 3, [sc in next st] twice; rep from * along entire lower edge of shawl.

BLOCKING

Soak shawl in warm water and pin to maximum size. Allow to dry.

FRINGE

Cut 3 strands of yarn 16"/40.5cm long. Holding 3 strands tog, fold in half and draw loop through 1 ch-3 space along lower edge of shawl, draw ends of strands through folded loop and pull to tighten. Rep in each ch-3 space along lower edge of shawl. Braid strands in each fringe, knotting the end of each braid. ◈

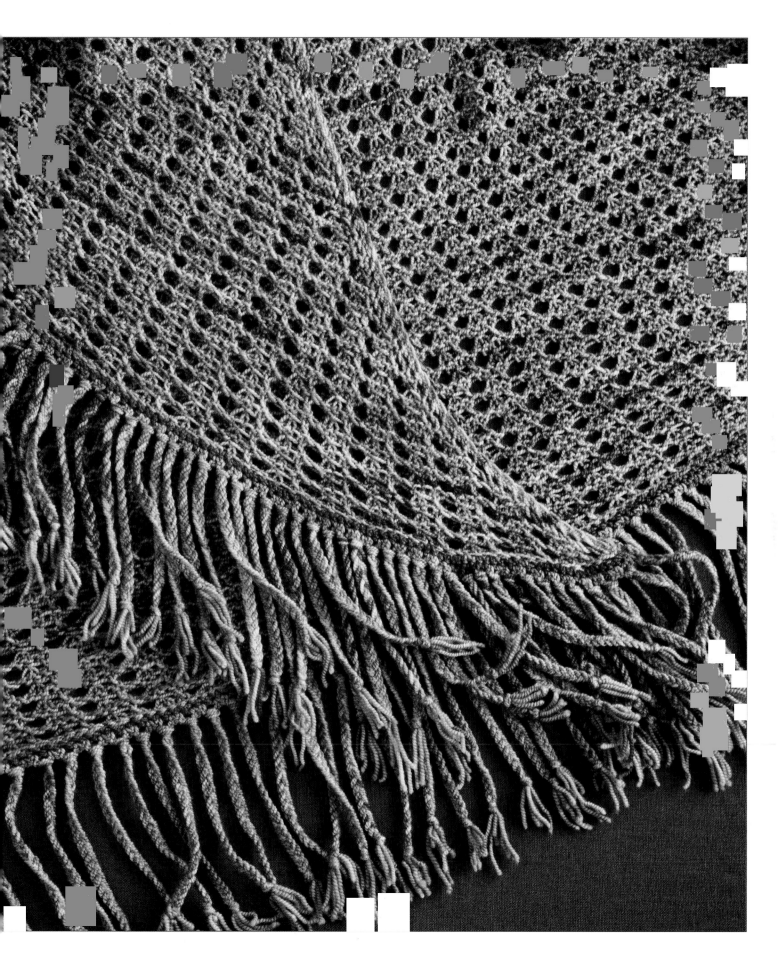

Metamorphosis Shrug

Wear this cleverly designed shrug as a flowing cocoon with cuffs
or as a sporty bolero with a draped cowl in the back.

MEASUREMENTS (after blocking)
◆ Width 52"/132cm
◆ Length 30"/76cm

MATERIALS
◆ Ten 1¾oz/50g skeins
(each 185yd/169m) of Koigu *Mori*
(mulberry silk/merino wool)
in #M312 **1**

◆ One pair size 3 (3.25mm) needles
or size to obtain gauge

GAUGE
26 stitches and 32 rows = 4"/10cm
over St st after blocking using
size 3 (3.25mm) needles.
TAKE TIME TO CHECK GAUGE.

STITCH GLOSSARY
Inc 1 K in back of st in row below the st
on needle, then k stitch on needle.

K1, P1 RIB
(over an odd number of sts)
Row 1 (RS) *K1, p1; rep from *, end k1.
Row 2 K the knit sts and p the purl sts.
Rep row 2 for k1, p1 rib.

LACE PATTERN
(over an even number of sts plus 3)
Row 1 (RS) K1, *k2tog;
rep from * to last 2 sts, k2.
Row 2 K2, *yo, k1tbl;
rep from * to last st, k1.
Rep rows 1–2 for lace pat.

NOTE
Shrug is worked from cuff to cuff in
one piece.

SHRUG
CUFF
Cast on 51 sts. Work in k1, p1 rib until
cuff measures 2"/5cm from beg.

BEGIN SHAPING
Inc row 1 (RS) [K2, inc 1] 17 times—68 sts.
Purl 1 row.

Metamorphosis Shrug

Inc row 2 [K2, inc 1] 22 times,
k to end—90 sts.
Purl 1 row.
Inc row 3 *K2, inc 1; rep from
* to end—120 sts.
Purl 1 row.
Rep last 2 rows once more—160 sts.
Inc row 4 (RS) *K3, inc 1; rep from * to
end—200 sts.
Purl 1 row.
Inc row 5 (RS) *Inc 1, k3; rep from * to
last st, inc 1—251 sts.
Purl 1 row. Piece measures approx
3½"/9cm.

BEGIN LACE PAT
Work in lace pat over 251 sts until piece
measures 47"/119cm from beg, end
with a WS row.

SHAPE CUFF
Dec row 1 (RS) *K2tog, k3; rep from * to
last st, k2tog—200 sts.
Purl 1 row.
Dec row 2 (RS) *K3, k2tog; rep from * to
end—160 sts.
Purl 1 row.
Dec row 3 (RS) *K2, k2tog; rep from * to
end—120 sts.
Purl 1 row.
Rep last 2 rows once more—90 sts.
Dec row 4 (RS) [K2, k2tog] 22 times,
k to end—68 sts.
Purl 1 row.
Dec row 5 (RS) [K2, k2tog] 17 times—51 sts.
Next row (WS) P1, *k1, p1; rep from * to end.
Cont in k1, p1 rib for 2"/5cm.
Bind off loosely.

FINISHING
BLOCKING
Soak shrug in warm water. Lay flat and
pin to measurements. Allow to dry.

Seam ribbed portion of each cuff.◈

●●●●

Gypsy

Complementary stitch patterns add both texture and lightness to a classic triangular shawl.

MEASUREMENTS
◆ Width 56"/142cm before blocking, 74"/188cm after blocking
◆ Length 24"/61cm before blocking, 26"/66cm after blocking

MATERIALS
◆ Five 1¾oz/50g skeins (each 175yd/161m) of Koigu *KPPPM* (merino wool) in #P105L (1)

◆ Size 3 (3mm) circular needle, 60"/152.4cm long (used to work back and forth), *or size to obtain gauge*

◆ Size E/4 (3.5mm) crochet hook

◆ Removable stitch marker

GAUGE
28 stitches and 36 rows = 4"/10cm over St st after blocking using size 3 (3.25mm) needles.
TAKE TIME TO CHECK GAUGE.

STITCH GLOSSARY
LI (lifted increase) Place RH needle behind LH needle and insert point from top to bottom into the purled top of the st in the row below the next st, knit, then knit the st above it.

RIGHT BORDER PATTERN
(worked at beg of RS rows and end of WS rows)
Row 1 (RS) Sl 1, k1, yo, k1, [yo, k2tog] 4 times.
Row 2 Purl.
Rep rows 1 and 2 for right border pat.

LEFT BORDER PATTERN
(worked at end of RS rows and beg of WS rows)
Row 1 (RS) [SKP, yo] 4 times, k1, yo, k2.
Row 2 Sl 1, p11.
Rep rows 1 and 2 for left border pat.

NOTE
Shawl is worked from the back neck edge to the lower point.

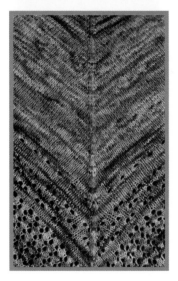

Gypsy

SHAWL

Cast on 9 sts. Place a marker on the center st, and move this marker up every row. Knit 1 row. Purl 1 row.

BEGIN CHART 1

Next row (RS) Work row 1 of chart to end—4 sts inc'd.
Cont to work chart in this way until row 12 is complete—33 sts.
Cont in pat as foll:
Next row (RS) Work right border, knit to one st before marked st, LI, k1, LI, knit to last 11 sts, work left border to end—4 sts inc'd.
Next row (WS) Work left border, p to end.
Rep last 2 rows 43 times more—209 sts.
Eyelet row (RS) Work right border, [k3, yo, k2tog, k1, SKP, yo] 11 times across, k4, LI, k1, LI, k4, [k3, yo, k2tog, k1, SKP, yo] 11 times, k4, work left border—4 sts inc'd.
Next row (WS) Work left border, p to end.
Next row (RS) Work right border, knit to one st before marked center st, LI, k1, LI, knit to last 11 sts, work left border to end—4 sts inc'd.
Next row (WS) Work left border, p to end.
Rep last 2 rows 3 times more—229 sts.

BEGIN CHART 2

Row 1 (RS) Work to red rep line, work 6-st rep 17 times across, work to next rep line, work 6-st rep 17 times across, work to end of chart—4 sts inc'd.
Cont to work chart in this manner until row 6 is complete—241 sts.
Next row (RS) Work right border, knit to one st before marked center st, LI, k1, LI, knit to last 11 sts, work left border to end—4 sts inc'd.
Next row (WS) Work left border, p to end.
Rep last 2 rows once more—249 sts.

BEGIN TRELLIS LACE CHART

Row 1 (RS) Work right border, yo, SK2P, yo, work 6-st trellis lace rep 18 times across, k1, LI, k1 (center st), LI, yo, SK2P, yo, work 6-st trellis lace rep 18 times across, k1, work left border—4 sts inc'd.
Row 2 Work left border, p to end.
Row 3 Work right border, k4, work 6-st trellis lace rep 18 times across, k to 1 st before marked st, LI, k1, LI, k4, work 6-st trellis lace rep 18 times across, yo, SK2P, yo, k to last 11 sts, work left border—4 sts inc'd.
Rep rows 1–4 of trellis lace, working inc'd sts into pat, for 4 times more—289 sts.
Next row (RS) Work right border, knit to one st before marked st, LI, k1, LI, knit to last 11 sts, work left border to end.
Next row (WS) Work left border, p to end.
Rep last 2 rows once more—297 sts.

BEGIN LITTLE ARROWHEADS CHART

Row 1 (RS) Work right border, k4, work 6-st rep 22 times across, LI, k1, LI, work 6-st rep 22 times across, k4, work left border. Cont to work chart in this manner, working inc's into pat, until row 4 is complete. Rep rows 1–4 four times more—337 sts.

Gypsy

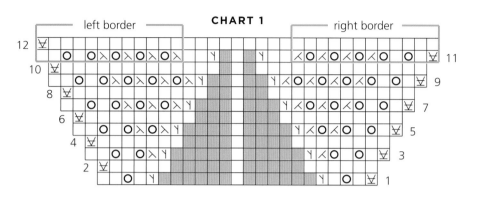

CHART 1

left border — right border

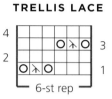

TRELLIS LACE

6-st rep

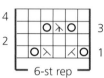

LITTLE ARROWHEADS

6-st rep

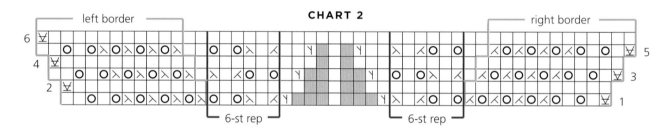

CHART 2

left border — right border

6-st rep — 6-st rep

FINISHING

BLOCKING
Soak shawl and pin to maximum size.
Allow to dry.

CROCHET TRIM
With crochet hook, work 1 row sc along
lower edge of shawl. Turn.
Next row *Ch 5, skip 3 sc, sc in next sc;
rep from * to end.
Next row *Ch 5, sc in ch-5 space;
rep from * to end.
Rep last row once more. Fasten off.

FRINGE
Cut 4 strands of yarn 13"/33cm long.
Holding 4 strands tog, fold in half and,
with crochet hook, draw loop through
one ch-5 space on lower edge of shawl.
Pull ends of strands through folded
loop, pull to tighten. Repeat along entire
lower edge of shawl.◈

STITCH KEY

☐ k on RS, p on WS

◩ k2tog

◪ SKP

Ⓞ yo

Ⓨ kfb

▦ no stitch

SK2P

slip 1 wyif

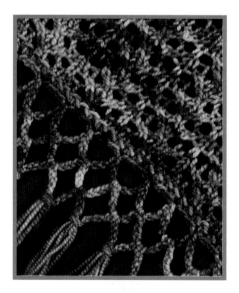

Woodsong

The lacework and pretty picot edge on this airy, sophisticated shawl are a symphony of design technique.

MEASUREMENTS (after blocking)
◆ Width at lower edge 67"/170cm
◆ Length 24"/61cm

MATERIALS
◆ Three 1¾oz/50g skeins (each 292yd/161m) of Koigu *Lace Merino* (wool) in #L170 **(0)**

◆ Size 6 (4mm) circular needle, 40"/101.5cm long (used to work back and forth), *or size to obtain gauge*

◆ Size G/6 (4mm) crochet hook (for provisional cast-on)

◆ Scrap yarn

◆ Cable needle (cn)

◆ Stitch markers

GAUGE
21 stitches and 16 rows = 4"/10cm over chart 2 after blocking using size 6 (4mm) needles.
TAKE TIME TO CHECK GAUGE.

PROVISIONAL CAST-ON
With scrap yarn and crochet hook, chain the number of stitches to cast on plus a few extra. Cut a tail and pull the tail through the last chain. With knitting needle and yarn, pick up and knit the stated number of stitches through the "purl bumps" on the back of the chain. To remove scrap chain, when instructed, pull out the tail from the last crochet stitch. Gently and slowly pull on the tail to unravel the crochet stitches, carefully placing each released knit stitch on a needle.

NOTE
Shawl is worked from the back neck tab to the lower edge.

Woodsong

SHAWL

TAB

Cast on 3 sts using provisional cast-on method. Knit 6 rows.

Next row (WS) Pick up and k 3 sts along edge of tab, remove scrap yarn and k 3 cast-on sts—9 sts.

Row 1 (RS) K3, M1, k3, M1, k3—11 sts.

Row 2 (inc) K3, *k1, yo; rep from * to last 3 sts, k3—16 sts.

Rows 3–5 Knit.

Row 6 Rep row 2—26 sts.

Rows 7–12 Knit.

Row 13 Rep row 2—46 sts.

Rows 14–18 Knit.

Row 19 K3, k1, *yo, k2tog; rep from * to last 4 sts, k4.

Rows 20–24 Knit.

Row 25 K3, *k1, yo; rep from * to last 3 sts, k3—86 sts.

Rows 26 and 27 Knit.

Row 28 Knit, inc 1 st in center of row—87 sts.

BEGIN CHART 1

Row 1 (RS) K5, work 7-st rep 11 times across, k5.

Row 2 (WS) K5, work 7-st rep 11 times across, k5.

Cont to work chart 1 in this manner until row 4 is complete. Rep rows 1–4 four times more.

Knit 4 rows.

Next (inc) row (RS) K3, yo, *k1, yo; rep from * to last 3 sts, k3—169 sts.

Knit 2 rows.

Next row (WS) K3, kfb, k to last 4 sts, kfb, k3—171 sts.

BEGIN CHART 2

Row 1 (RS) K3, work 14-st rep 11 times across, work to end of chart, k3.

Row 2 (WS) K3, work to rep line, work 14-st rep 11 times across, k3.

Cont to work chart in this manner until row 8 is complete. Rep rows 1–8 four times more.

Next row (RS) K3, kfb, k to last 4 sts, kfb, k3—173 sts.

Knit 1 row.

Next (inc) row (RS) K3, yo, *k1, yo; rep from * to last 3 sts, k3—341 sts.

Knit 2 rows.

BEGIN CHART 3

Set-up row (WS) K2, work to rep line, work 28-st rep 12 times across, k2.

Row 1 (RS) K2, work 28-st rep 12 times across, work to end of chart, k2.

Cont to work chart in this manner until row 18 is complete. Rep rows 1–18 three times more, then rows 1–17 once.

Knit 3 rows.

Next row (RS) K1, *k2tog, yo; rep from * to last 2 sts, k2.

Knit 3 rows.

Bind off using picot bind-off method as foll: K1, *return st to LH needle, cast on 2 sts, bind off 4 sts, rep from * until all sts have been bound off.

FINISHING

BLOCKING

Soak in tepid water and pin to measurements, keeping half-circle shape Allow to dry.◈

Woodsong

CHART 1

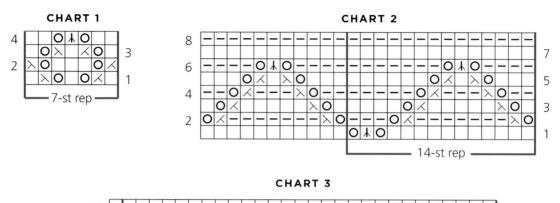

7-st rep

CHART 2

14-st rep

CHART 3

28-st rep

set-up row

STITCH KEY

☐ k on RS, p on WS

⊟ p on RS, k on WS

◸ k2tog

◿ SKP

◉ yo

⟁ S2KP

Corinne

A looped edging complements oversize cables while adding
a bit of whimsy to this luxuriously plush cape.

MEASUREMENTS
◆ Width along lower edge 85¼"/216.5cm
◆ Length not including edging 17½"/44cm

MATERIALS
◆ Six 3½oz/100g skeins
(each 93yd/85m) of Koigu *Bulky Merino*
(merino wool) in B72 ⑤

◆ Size 13 (9mm) circular needle,
32"/80cm long (used to work back and
forth), *or size to obtain gauge*

◆ Cable needle (cn)

◆ Size M/13 (9mm) crochet hook
for edging

◆ 6 stitch markers

GAUGE
10 stitches and 15 rows = 4"/10cm
over St st using size 13 (9mm) needle.
TAKE TIME TO CHECK GAUGE.

STITCH GLOSSARY
kfb Knit into the front and back of the next
st to inc 1 st.
pfb Purl into the front and back of next st
to inc 1 st.
sc3tog Insert crochet hook into next 3 sts
on needle, dropping sts off needle (4 loops
on hook), yo and draw a loop through
the 3 sts (2 loops on hook), yo and draw
through a loop to complete the sc.
4-st RC Sl 2 sts to cn and hold to *back*,
k2, k2 from cn.

3-st RPC Sl next st to cn and hold to *back*,
k2, p1 from cn.
3-st LPC Sl next 2 sts to cn and hold to
front, p1, k2 from cn.

SHAWL
Make a loop of yarn around your finger
for an adjustable ring cast-on. Work with
needle into loop on finger as follows:
([K1, yo] 4 times, k1) into the loop—9 sts.
Next row (WS) P1, [pfb] 7 times, p1—16 sts.
Next row Kfb in each st across—32 sts.
Next row [P8, place marker (pm)]
3 times, p8.

Corinne

BEGIN CABLE PAT

Set-up row 1 (RS) [P2, 4-st RC, p2, sl marker, yo, pm] 3 times, p2, 4-st RC, p2.

Next row [K2, p4, k2, sl marker, yo, sl marker] 3 times, k2, p4, k2—35 sts.

Set-up row 2 [P1, 3-st RPC, 3-st LPC, p1, sl marker, yo, k1, yo, sl marker] 3 times, p1, 3-st RPC, 3-st LPC, p1—41 sts.

Next row [K1, p2, k2, p2, k1, sl marker, p to next marker, sl marker] 3 times, k1, p2, k2, p2, k1.

BEGIN CHART

Row 1 (RS) [Work chart over 8 sts, sl marker, yo, k to next marker, yo, sl marker] 3 times, work chart over 8 sts—6 sts inc'd.

Row 2 [Work chart over 8 sts, sl marker, p to next marker, sl marker] 3 times, work chart over 8 sts.

Cont to work in this manner until row 12 of chart is complete, rep rows 1–12 three times more, then rep rows 1–10 once—215 sts. Do not bind off. Do not cut yarn.

FINISHING

CROCHET EDGE

With RS facing, place first st on crochet hook, *ch 8, sc3tog, rep from * to last st, ch 8, place last st on hook, yo and draw through a loop, yo and draw through both loops on hook. Fasten off.◈

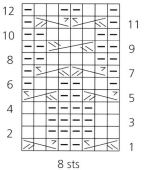

STITCH KEY

☐ k on RS, p on WS

— p on RS, k on WS

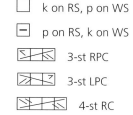 3-st RPC

3-st LPC

4-st RC

8 sts

Silver Lace

Subtly variegated cool hues and optional silver beads
complement a delicate allover lace pattern.

MEASUREMENTS
◆ Width 18"/45.5cm
◆ Length 64"/162.5cm

MATERIALS
◆ Five 1¾oz/50g skeins
(each 175yd/161m) of Koigu *KPPPM*
(merino wool) in #P343 (**1**)

◆ One pair size 6 (4mm) needles
or size to obtain gauge

◆ Size D/3 (3.25mm) crochet hook

◆ Approx 200 silver beads #6 (optional)

GAUGE
20 stitches and 24 rows = 4"/10cm
over St st after blocking using
size 6 (4mm) needles.
TAKE TIME TO CHECK GAUGE.

LACE PATTERN
(multiple of 8 sts plus 13)
Row 1 (RS) K5, *k2tog, yo, k6;
rep from * to end.
Row 2 Purl.
Row 3 K5, *yo, k3tog, yo, k5;
rep from * to end.
Row 4 Purl.
Row 5 K4, *yo, k2tog, k1, k2tog, yo, k3;
rep from * to last st, k1.
Row 6 P5, *yo, p3tog, yo, p5;
rep from * to end.
Row 7 Knit.
Row 8 P3, *yo, p2tog, p3, p2tog, yo, p1;
rep from * to last 2 sts, p2.
Row 9 K4, *yo, k2tog, k1, k2tog, yo, k3;
rep from * to last st, k1.

Row 10 P5, *yo, p3tog, yo, p5;
rep from * to end.
Row 11 Knit.
Row 12 P3, *p2tog, yo, p3, yo, p2tog, p1;
rep from * to last 2 sts, p2.
Row 13 K2, k2tog, yo, *k5, yo, k3tog, yo;
rep from * to last 9 sts, k5, yo, k2tog, k2.
Row 14 Purl.
Rep rows 1–14 for lace pat.

Silver Lace

NOTES
1. Lace pattern may be worked from text or chart.
2. If desired, add beads in row 10 of lace pat or chart, by slipping bead onto every other p3tog as it is completed, then placing the beaded st back on the RH needle.

SHAWL
Cast on 77 sts. Knit 2 rows.

BEGIN LACE CHART
Row 1 (RS) Work chart row to rep line, work 8-st rep 8 times across, work to end of chart row.
Cont to work chart in this way through row 14, adding beads if desired in row 10 (see note). Rep rows 1–14 until shawl measures approx 61"/155cm from beg, end with a row 14.
Knit 2 rows. Bind off.

FINISHING
EDGING
Join yarn to side edge of shawl.
Row 1 *Sc in edge st, ch 1; rep from * along edge of shawl, sc in last edge st, ch 3, turn.

Next (picot) row Ch 3, sl st in 3rd ch from hook, *(sc in next ch sp, ch 3, adding bead in 2nd ch if desired, sc in same ch-sp), sc in next ch space; rep from * to end. Fasten off. Rep for 2nd side edge of shawl.

BORDER
Join yarn at corner, work 71 sc evenly along cast-on edge of shawl.
Next row Turn, ch 5, *sk next 2 sc, sc in next sc, sk 3 sc, ch 5, rep from *, end with sc in last sc.
Next (picot) row Turn, *ch 5, (sc, ch 3, adding bead in 2nd ch, sc) in ch-5 sp, rep from *, end sc in last ch-sp.
Rep picot row 3 times more. Fasten off. Rep for bound-off edge.

BLOCKING
Wet shawl and pin to measurements. Allow to dry.◈

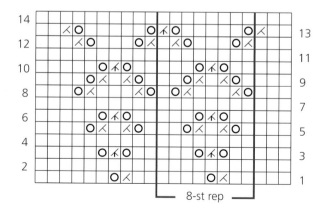

STITCH KEY

☐ k on RS, p on WS

▨ k2tog on RS, p2tog on WS

Ｏ yo

▨ k3tog on RS, p3tog on WS

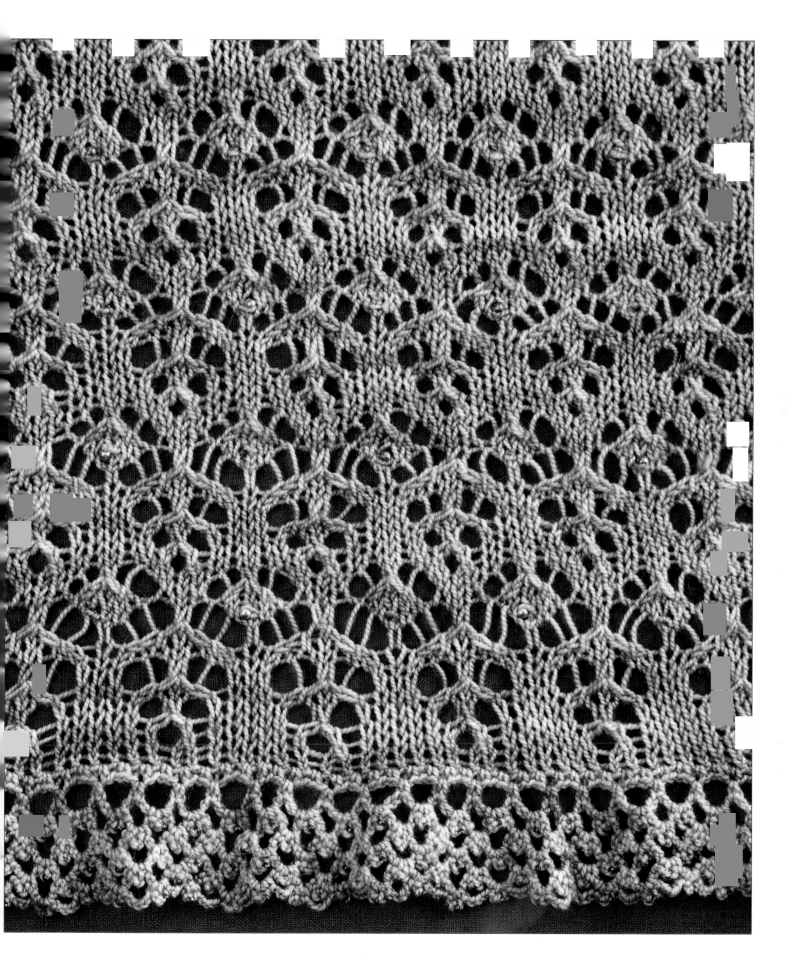

Keepsake

A keepsake of many colors: a square shawl that can double as a throw is knit in stripes of twelve colorways.

MEASUREMENTS (after blocking)
◆ 60 x 60"/152 x 152cm

MATERIALS
◆ One 1¾oz/50g skein
(each 175yd/161m) of Koigu *KPPPM*
(merino wool) each in #P612 (A),
#P816 (B), #P511L (C), #P814 (D),
#P605 (E), #P608 (F), #P621 (G),
#P513 (H), #P602 (I), #P628 (J),
#P623 (K), and #P324 (L)

◆ Size 6 (4mm) circular needle,
60"/152.4cm long (used to work back and
forth), *or size to obtain gauge*

◆ Size G/6 (4mm) crochet hook

◆ Stitch marker

GAUGE
24 stitches and 30 rows = 4"/10cm
over St st using size 6 (4mm) needles.
TAKE TIME TO CHECK GAUGE.

STRIPE SEQUENCE
[2 rows B, 2 rows A] twice, 12 rows B.
[2 rows C, 2 rows B] twice, 12 rows C.
[2 rows D, 2 rows C] twice, 12 rows D.
[2 rows E, 2 rows D] twice, 12 rows E.
[2 rows F, 2 rows E] twice, 12 rows F.
[2 rows G, 2 rows F] twice, 12 rows G.
[2 rows H, 2 rows G] twice, 12 rows H.
[2 rows I, 2 rows H] twice, 12 rows I.
[2 rows J, 2 rows I] twice, 12 rows J.
[2 rows K, 2 rows J] twice, 12 rows K.
[2 rows L, 2 rows K] twice, 12 rows L.
Rep stripe sequence from
beginning to end.

Keepsake

SHAWL

With A, cast on 399 sts loosely. Place marker in center st. Knit 2 rows.

Set-up row 1 Work to first rep line, work 9-st rep 20 times across, work to beg of next 9-st rep, work 9-st rep 20 times across, work to end of chart.
Work set-up row 2 in this manner.
Cont to work chart in this way until row 12 is complete.

BEGIN STRIPE SEQUENCE

Cont to work chart pat as established until row 18 is complete. Working in stripe sequence, rep rows 1–18 until 5 sts rem. Note that you will be working 1 less 9-st rep on each side of center st as each 18-row rep is complete.
Next row (WS) P1, k4.

Next (dec) row K2tog, k1, SKP.
Next row K3tog. Fasten off.

FINISHING
CROCHET EDGING

With hook and any color, work 1 row sc around entire edge of shawl.

BLOCKING

Soak shawl in warm water and pin to maximum size. Allow to dry.

FRINGE

Using colors randomly, cut 6 strands of yarn 12"/30.5cm long. Holding 6 strands tog, fold in half and with crochet hook, draw loop through 1 sc in edge of shawl. Rep along lower edge of shawl, adding fringe in every 6th sc. ◆

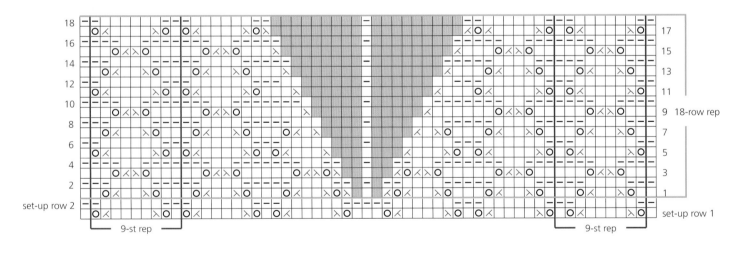

STITCH KEY

☐ k on RS, p on WS

⊟ p on RS, k on WS

◩ k2tog

◩ SKP

◉ yo

▨ no stitch

Tabitha

A wide expanse of stockinette stitch provides a showcase for the subtle variations of a tonal colorway.

MEASUREMENTS (after blocking)
◆ Width from top edge to center point 25"/63.5cm
◆ Length across top edge 78"/198cm

MATERIALS
◆ Seven 1¾oz/50g skeins (each 114yd/100m) of Koigu *Kersti* (merino wool crepe) in #K637 (3)

◆ One pair size 7 (4.5mm) needles *or size to obtain gauge*

◆ Size 7 (4.5mm) circular needle, 24"/60cm long

◆ Stitch markers

GAUGE
22 stitches and 26 rows = 4"/10cm over St st after blocking using size 7 (4.5mm) needles.
TAKE TIME TO CHECK GAUGE.

NOTE
Shawl is worked from end to end.

SHAWL
Cast on 14 sts.
Next row (WS) Knit.
Row 1 (RS) K5, yo, ssk, place marker (pm), yo, pm, k2, yo, ssk, k3—15 sts.
Row 2 and all WS rows K3, p2, yo, p2tog, sl marker, p to the next marker, sl marker, p2, yo, p2tog, k3.
Row 3 K5, yo, ssk, sl marker, k to the next marker, yo, sl marker, k2, yo, ssk, k3—1 st inc'd.
Rep last 2 rows until piece measures approx 36"/91.5cm from beg, or until half

the yarn has been used, end with a WS row.
Next row (RS) Work in pat over 7 sts, sl marker, k to 3 sts before next marker, k3tog, yo, sl marker, work in pat over 7 sts—1 st dec'd.
Next row Rep row 2.
Rep last 2 rows until 3 sts rem between markers, end with a WS row.
Next row Work in pat over 7 sts, k3tog, work in pat over 7 sts—15 sts.
Bind off.

FINISHING
Block to measurements. ◈

Kiki

Striking, striped zigzag lace balances the weight of a bulky
yarn that envelops you like a warm embrace.

MEASUREMENTS
- ◆ Width across top edge 69¾"/177cm
- ◆ Length from top edge to point 39"/99cm

MATERIALS
- ◆ Two 3½oz/100g skeins
(each 93yd/85m) of Koigu *Bulky Merino*
(merino wool) in #B30 (B) ⑤

- ◆ One skein each in #B70 (A),
#B60 (C), and #B20 (D)

- ◆ Size 15 (10mm) circular needle,
32"/81cm long (used to work back and
forth), *or size to obtain gauge*

- ◆ Size N/15 (10mm) crochet hook

GAUGE
7 stitches and 12 rows = 4"/10cm
over zigzag lace pattern using
size 15 (10mm) needle.
TAKE TIME TO CHECK GAUGE.

ZIGZAG LACE PATTERN
(over an even number of sts)
Rows 1, 3, and 5 (RS) K1, *yo, k2tog;
rep from * to last st, k1.
Row 2 and all WS rows Purl.
Rows 7, 9, and 11 K1, *SKP, yo;
rep from * to last st, k1.
Row 12 Rep row 2.
Rep rows 1–12 for zigzag lace pat.

SHAWL
With A, cast on 4 sts.
Work rows 1 and 2 in zigzag lace pat. Cont
in pat as established, inc 1 st each side
every other row, working incs into zigzag
lace pat, until piece measures 7"/18cm
from beg, end with a WS row.

Cont in this manner, working color
sequence as foll: 12 rows B, 12 rows A, 12
rows B, 12 rows C, [12 rows B, 12 rows D]
twice. Bind off. Do not break yarn.

FINISHING
With crochet hook and D, work one row
of sl st along bound-off edge. Fasten off.
With crochet hook and B, work sc along
all rem edges, working 3 sc into point.
Fasten off.◈

Cobweb

Weave a web of lightweight luxury with a diaphanous stole that serves as a chic outer layer.

MEASUREMENTS (after blocking)
◆ Width 30¾"/78cm
◆ Length 72"/183cm

MATERIALS
◆ Four 1¾oz/50g skeins (each 292yd/267m) of Koigu *Lace Merino* (merino wool) in #L366 〖0〗

◆ Size 6 (4mm) needles *or size to obtain gauge*

GAUGE
13 stitches and 14 rows = 4"/10cm using size 6 (4mm) needles over pattern st after blocking.
TAKE TIME TO CHECK GAUGE.

PATTERN STITCH
(multiple of 4 sts)
Row 1 *K2tog, yo, k2; rep from * across.
Rep row 1 for pat st.

SHAWL
Cast on 100 sts. Knit 1 row, purl 1 row for St st.

BEGIN PAT ST
Work in pat st until piece measures approx 72"/183cm. Work 2 rows in St st. Bind off very loosely.

FINISHING
BLOCKING
Wet shawl and pin to measurements. Allow to dry.◈

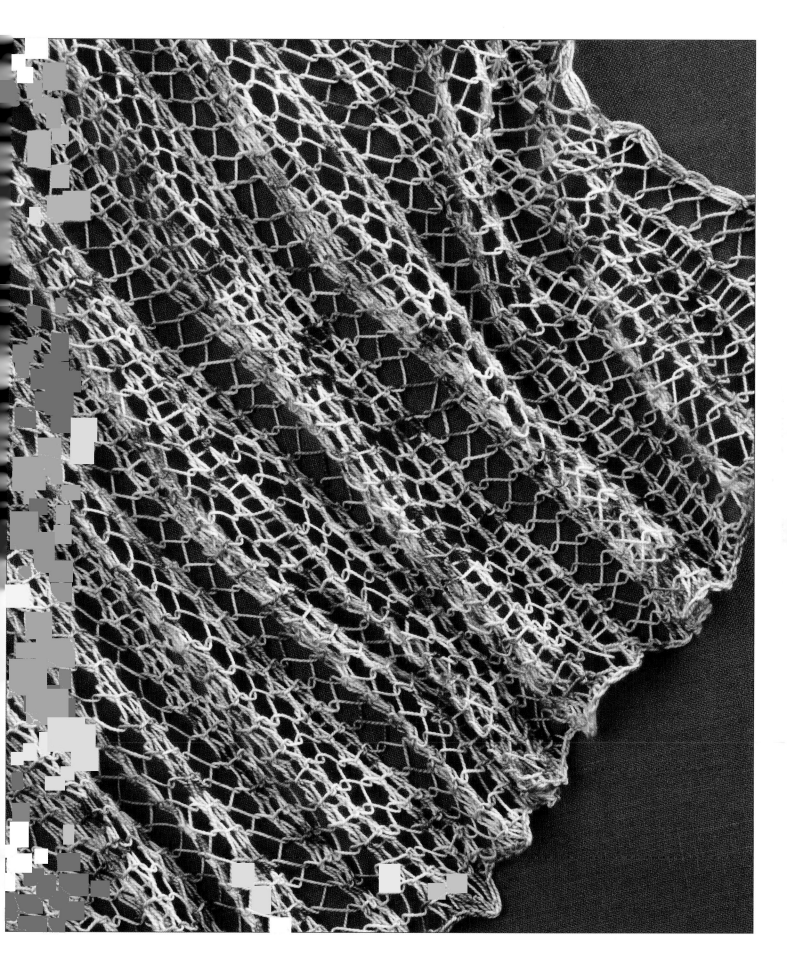

Lola

A simple garter stripe pattern in a mix of bulky and fingering weights produces a springy, eye-catching fabric that's as comfy as your favorite blanket.

MEASUREMENTS (unstretched)
◆ Width 40"/101.5cm
◆ Length 63"/160cm

MATERIALS
◆ Eight 3½oz/100g skeins (each approx 93yd/85m) of Koigu *Bulky Merino* (merino wool) in #B1075 (A) **⑤**

◆ Four 1¾oz/50g skeins (each approx 175yd/160m) of Koigu *KPPPM* (merino wool) in #P133A (B) **❶**

◆ Size 15 (10mm) circular needle, 24"/61cm long (used to work back and forth), *or size to obtain gauge*

GAUGE
10 stitches and 19 rows = 4"/10cm over twisted garter stripe pat using size 15 (10mm) needle and A.
TAKE TIME TO CHECK GAUGE.

TWISTED GARTER STRIPE PATTERN
(over any number of sts)
Rows 1–4 With A, ktbl.
Rows 5–8 With B, ktbl.
Rep rows 1–8 for twisted garter stripe pat.

NOTE
Shawl will stretch when worn.

SHAWL
With A, cast on 100 sts.
Rep rows 1–8 of twisted garter stripe pat 29 times. Rep rows 1–4 once more.
With A, bind off. ◆

Rihanna

Lace patterns fan out from a vertical center line to form a triangular shawl with pretty crochet trim.

MEASUREMENTS (after blocking)
◆ Width along upper edge 48"/122cm
◆ Length not including crochet trim 29"/73.5cm

MATERIALS
◆ Four 1¾oz/50g skeins (each 175yd/160m) of Koigu *KPPPM* (merino wool) in #P611 [1]

◆ Size 6 (4mm) circular needle, 24"/60cm long (used to work back and forth), *or size to obtain gauge*

◆ Size C/2 (2.75mm) crochet hook

◆ Stitch markers

GAUGE
14 stitches and 25 rows = 4"/10cm over lace pattern after blocking using size 6 (4mm) needle.
TAKE TIME TO CHECK GAUGE.

SEED STITCH
(over an odd number of sts)
Row 1 (RS) *K1, p1; rep from * to last st, k1.
Row 2 P the knit sts and k the purl sts.
Rep row 2 for seed st.

SHAWL
Cast on 15 sts.

BEGIN CHART 1
Row 1 (RS) Sl 1 wyif, work 5 seed sts, work chart row to last 6 sts, work 5 seed sts, k1—4 sts inc'd.
Row 2 Sl 1 wyif, work 5 seed sts, work chart row to last 6 sts, work 5 seed sts, k1.
Cont to work chart in this way until row 12 is complete—39 sts.

Next row (RS) Sl 1, work 5 seed sts, work chart row 7 to rep line, work 6-st rep twice, work to next rep line, work 6-st rep twice, work to end of chart row, work 5 seed sts, k1—43 sts.
Cont to work chart in this way until row 12 is complete—51 sts. Rep rows 7–12 for 18 times more—267 sts.

Rihanna

BEGIN CHART 2

Row 1 (RS) Sl 1, work 5 seed sts, work chart row to rep line, work 6-st rep 21 times across, work to end of chart row, k1, work chart row to rep line, work 6-st rep 21 times across, work to end of chart row, work 5 seed sts, k1.

Cont to work chart in this way until row 16 is complete—299 sts. Do not bind off. Do not break yarn.

FINISHING

CROCHET TRIM

With RS facing, place first st on crochet hook, *ch 8, work as foll: insert crochet hook in next st, and draw through a loop, letting knit st drop from needle, yo and draw through 2 loops to complete the sc; rep from * to end. Fasten off.

Sew cast-on edge together to form a straight edge.
Block knitted fabric gently, omitting the crochet trim.◈

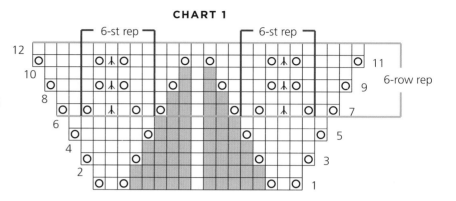

CHART 1

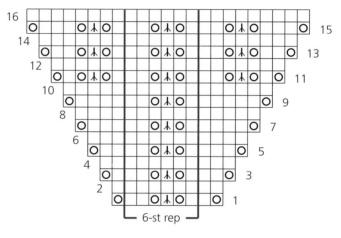

CHART 2

STITCH KEY

☐ k on RS, p on WS

▣ yo

⊼ S2KP

▨ no stitch

Terms & Techniques

Abbreviations

approx	approximately
beg	begin(ning)
CC	contrasting color
ch	chain
cm	centimeter(s)
cn	cable needle
cont	continu(e)(ing)
dec	decreas(e)(ing)
dpn(s)	double-pointed needle(s)
foll	follow(s)(ing)
g	gram(s)
inc	increas(e)(ing)
k	knit
kfb	knit into the front and back of a stitch—one stitch has been increased
k2tog	knit 2 stitches together—one stitch has been decreased
LH	left-hand
lp(s)	loop(s)
m	meter(s)
mm	millimeter(s)
MC	main color
M1 or M1L	make one or make one left (see glossary)
M1 p-st	make one purl stitch (see glossary)
M1R	make one right (see glossary)
oz	ounce(s)
p	purl
pfb	purl into front and back of a stitch—one stitch has been increased
pat(s)	pattern(s)
pm	place marker
psso	pass slip stitch(es) over
p2tog	purl two stitches together—one stitch has been decreased
rem	remain(s)(ing)
rep	repeat
RH	right-hand
RS	right side(s)
rnd(s)	round(s)
SKP	slip 1, knit 1, pass slip stitch over—one stitch has been decreased
SK2P	slip 1, knit 2 together, pass slip stitch over the k2tog—two stitches decreased
S2KP	slip 2 stitches together, knit 1, pass 2 slip stitches over knit 1
sc	single crochet
sl	slip
sl st	slip stitch
spp	slip, purl, pass sl st over
ssk(ssp)	slip 2 sts knitwise one at a time, insert LH needle through fronts of sts and knit (purl) together
sssk	slip 3 sts one at a time knitwise, insert LH needle through fronts of sts and knit together
st(s)	stitch(es)
St st	stockinette stitch
tbl	through back loop(s)
tog	together
WS	wrong side(s)
wyib	with yarn in back
wyif	with yarn in front
yd(s)	yd(s)
yo	yarn over needle
*	repeat directions following * as indicated
[ ]	repeat directions inside brackets as indicated

Skill Levels

● ○ ○ ○
Beginner
Ideal first project.

_____

● ● ○ ○
Easy
Basic stitches, minimal shaping, and simple finishing.

_____

● ● ● ○
Intermediate
For knitters with some experience. More intricate stitches, shaping, and finishing.

_____

● ● ● ●
Experienced
For knitters able to work patterns with complicated shaping and finishing.

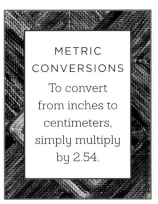

METRIC CONVERSIONS
To convert from inches to centimeters, simply multiply by 2.54.

Glossary

bind off Used to finish an edge or segment. Lift the first stitch over the second, the second over the third, etc. (U.K.: cast off)

bind off in rib or pat Work in rib or pat as you bind off. (Knit the knit stitches, purl the purl stitches.)

cast on Place a foundation row of stitches upon the needle in order to begin knitting.

decrease Reduce the stitches in a row (for example, knit two together).

increase Add stitches in a row (for example, knit in front and back of stitch).

knitwise Insert the needle into the stitch as if you were going to knit it.

make one or make one left Insert left-hand needle from front to back under the strand between last st worked and next st on left-hand needle. Knit into the back loop to twist the stitch.

make one p-st Insert needle from front to back under the strand between the last stitch worked and the next stitch on the left-hand needle. Purl into the back loop to twist the stitch.

make one right Insert left-hand needle from back to front under the strand between the last stitch worked and the next stitch on left-hand needle. Knit into the front loop to twist the stitch.

no stitch On some charts, "no stitch" is indicated with shaded spaces where stitches have been decreased or not yet made. In such cases, work the stitches of the chart, skipping over the "no stitch" spaces.

place marker Place or attach a loop of contrast yarn or purchased stitch marker as indicated.

pick up and knit (purl) Knit (or purl) into the loops along an edge.

purlwise Insert the needle into the stitch as if you were going to purl it.

selvage stitch Edge stitch that helps make seaming easier.

slip, slip, knit Slip next two stitches knitwise, one at a time, to right-hand needle. Insert tip of left-hand needle into fronts of these stitches, from left to right. Knit them together. One stitch has been decreased.

slip, slip, slip, knit Slip next three stitches knitwise, one at a time, to right-hand needle. Insert tip of left-hand needle into fronts of these stitches, from left to right. Knit them together. Two stitches have been decreased.

slip stitch An unworked stitch made by passing a stitch from the left-hand to the right-hand needle as if to purl.

work even Continue in pattern without increasing or decreasing. (U.K.: work straight)

yarn over Make a new stitch by wrapping the yarn over the right-hand needle. (U.K.: yfwd, yon, yrn)

Needle Sizes

U.S.	Metric
0	2mm
1	2.25mm
2	2.75mm
3	3.25mm
4	3.5mm
5	3.75mm
6	4mm
7	4.5mm
8	5mm
9	5.5mm
10	6mm
10½	6.5mm
11	8mm
13	9mm
15	10mm
17	12.75mm
19	15mm
35	19mm

page 100

Standard Yarn Weight System

Catagories of yarn, gauge ranges, and recommended needle and hook sizes

Yarn Weight Symbol & Category Names	0 Lace	1 Super Fine	2 Fine	3 Light	4 Medium	5 Bulky	6 Super Bulky
Type of Yarns in Category	Fingering 10 count crochet thread	Sock, Fingering, Baby	Sport, Baby	DK, Light Worsted	Worsted, Afghan, Aran	Chunky, Craft, Rug	Bulky, Roving
Knit Gauge Range* in Stockinette Stitch to 4 inches	33 –40** sts	27–32 sts	23–26 sts	21–24 sts	16–20 sts	12–15 sts	6–11 sts
Recommended Needle in Metric Size Range	1.5–2.25 mm	2.25–3.25 mm	3.25–3.75 mm	3.75–4.5 mm	4.5–5.5 mm	5.5–8 mm	8 mm and larger
Recommended Needle U.S. Size Range	000 to 1	1 to 3	3 to 5	5 to 7	7 to 9	9 to 11	11 and larger
Crochet Gauge* Ranges in Single Crochet to 4 inch	32-42 double crochets**	21–32 sts	16–20 sts	12–17 sts	11–14 sts	8–11 sts	5–9 sts
Recommended Hook in Metric Size Range	Steel*** 1.6–1.4mm Regular hook 2.25 mm	2.25–3.5 mm	3.5–4.5 mm	4.5–5.5 mm	5.5–6.5 mm	6.5–9 mm	9 mm and larger
Recommended Hook U.S. Size Range	Steel*** 6, 7, 8 Regular hook B–1	B–1 to E–4	E–4 to 7	7 to I–9	I–9 to K–10½	K–10½ to M–13	M–13 and larger

page 16

* GUIDELINES ONLY: The above reflect the most commonly used gauges and needle or hook sizes for specific yarn categories.

** Lace weight yarns are usually knitted or crocheted on larger needles and hooks to created lacy openwork patterns. Accordingly, a gauge range is difficult to determine. Always follow the gauge stated in your pattern.

*** Steel crochet hooks are sized differently from regular hooks—the higher the number, the smaller the hook, which is the reverse of regular hook sizing. This Standards & Guidelines booklet and downloadable symbol artwork are available at: YarnStandards.com

Crochet Chain

1. Draw the yarn through the loop on the hook by catching it with the hook and pulling it toward you.

2. One chain stitch is complete. Lightly tug on the yarn to tighten the loop if it is very loose, or wiggle the hook to loosen the loop if it is very tight. Repeat from step 1 to make as many chain stitches as required for your pattern.

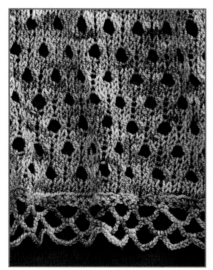

page 30

Single Crochet

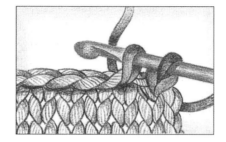

1. Draw through a loop as for a slip stitch, bring the yarn over the hook, and pull it through the first loop. *Insert the hook into the next stitch and draw through a second loop.

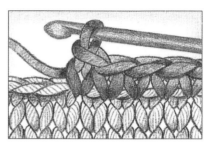

2. Yarn over and pull through both loops on the hook. Repeat from the * to the end.

Picking Up Stitches

ALONG A HORIZONTAL EDGE:
1. Insert the knitting needle into the center of the first stitch in the row below the bound-off edge. Wrap the yarn knitwise around the needle.

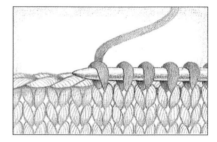

2. Draw the yarn through. You have picked up one stitch. Continue to pick up one stitch in each stitch along the bound-off edge.

ALONG A VERTICAL EDGE:
1. Insert the knitting needle into the corner stitch of the first row, one stitch in from the side edge. Wrap the yarn around the needle knitwise.

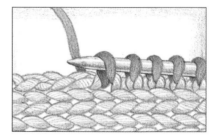

2. Draw the yarn through. You have picked up one stitch. Continue to pick up stitches along the edge. Occasionally skip one row to keep the edge from flaring.

Yarn Overs

A yarn over is a decorative increase made by wrapping the yarn around the needle. There are various ways to make a yarn over, depending on where it is placed.

BETWEEN TWO KNIT STITCHES:
Bring the yarn from the back of the work to the front between the two needles. Knit the next stitch, bringing the yarn to the back over the right-hand needle, as shown.

BETWEEN TWO PURL STITCHES:
Leave the yarn at the front of the work. Bring the yarn to the back over the right-hand needle and to the front again, as shown. Purl the next stitch.

BETWEEN A KNIT AND A PURL STITCH:
Bring the yarn from the back to the front between the two needles. Then bring it to the back over the right-hand needle and back to the front again, as shown. Purl the next stitch.

BETWEEN A PURL AND A KNIT STITCH:
Leave the yarn at the front of the work. Knit the next stitch, bringing the yarn to the back over the right-hand needle, as shown.

MULTIPLE YARN OVERS (TWO OR MORE):
Wrap the yarn around the needle, as when working a single yarn over, then continue wrapping the yarn around the needle as many times as indicated. Work the next stitch of the left-hand needle. On the following row, work stitches into the extra yarn overs, as described in the pattern. The illustration at right depicts a finished yarn over on the purl side.

Cables

Note: Cables shown are 6-stitch cables (3 sts on each side).
Twists are made with 2 stitches (1 on each side). Stitch glossaries in each pattern specify stitch counts for cables used in that pattern.

FRONT (OR LEFT) CABLE
1. Slip the first 3 stitches of the cable purlwise to a cable needle and hold them to the front of the work. Be careful not to twist the stitches.

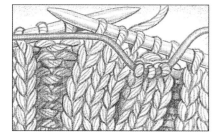

2. Leave the stitches suspended in front of the work, keeping them in the center of the cable needle, where they won't slip off.
Pull the yarn firmly and knit the next 3 stitches.

3. Knit the 3 stitches from the cable needle. If this seems too awkward, return the stitches to the left needle and then knit them.

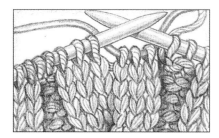

BACK (OR RIGHT) CABLE
1. Slip the first 3 stitches of the cable purlwise to a cable needle and hold them to the back of the work. Be careful not to twist the stitches.

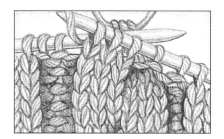

2. Leave the stitches suspended in back of the work, keeping them in the center of the cable needle, where they won't slip off.
Pull the yarn firmly and knit the next 3 stitches.

3. Knit the 3 stitches from the cable needle. If this seems too awkward, return the stitches to the left needle and then knit them.

Acknowledgments

To friends, to family, and to knitters who continue to inspire the Koigu journey: We thank you for the help, support, wisdom, guidance, and inspiration. Thank you to Trisha Malcolm and the Sixth&Spring Books team for making this book possible. To all our yarn stores, who make Koigu yarns and patterns available to the knitting world: thank you.

Resources

For a list of select shops in the United States, Canada, and overseas, please write to the below address or visit our website.

KOIGU WOOL DESIGNS
Box 158
Chatsworth, Ontario N0H 1G0
Canada
519-794-3066
www.koigu.com

FOLLOW US ON:
Facebook
Twitter
tumblr
instagram
Pinterest

Further Readings

Kempner, Beryl. *The Harmony Guide to Knitting as a Creative Craft*. London: Lyric Books Limited, 1991.

Landra, Maie. *Knits from a Painter's Palette*. New York: Sixth&Spring Books, 2006.

Matthews, Anne. *Vogue Dictionary of Knitting Stitches*. New York: William Morrow, 1985.

Miller, Sharon. *Heirloom Knitting*. Lerwick, Shetland, UK: Shetland Times, Ltd, 2002.

Reimann, Leili. *Pitsilised Koekirjad* (Koekirjad Lace). Tallinn, Estonia: Valgus, 1986.

Index

A

abbreviations 105
acknowledgments 111
Alligator 16–17
Allusion 41–43

C

cables 109
Charlotte's Daughter Joy 38–40
Charlotte's Daughter Nellie 12–15
Charlotte's Web 25–29
Cobweb 98–99
Corinne 84–86
crochet chain 107
crochet, single 107

D

Dash 53–55

E

Elizabeth 66–68

F

further readings 111

G

glossary 106
Groovy 44–45
Gypsy 75–78

K

Keepsake 90–93
Kiki 96–97

L

Lola 100–101
Lucky Lady 56–60

M

Maria 69–71
Metamorphosis Shrug 72–74
metric conversion 106

N

needle sizes 105

P

Patch of Berries 36–37
Peek-a-Boo 30–31
picking up stitches 107

R

resources 110
Rhapsody in Color 18–20
Rihanna 102–104

S

Silver Lace 87–89
skill levels 105
Starfish 32–35
Stroke of Midnight 64–65

T

Tabitha 94–95
Tumble Leaves 49–52

V

Valentina 21–24
Victoria 61–63

W

Waves 46–48
Woodsong 79–83

Y

yarn overs 108
yarn weights, standard 106